The

Last of the Peshwas

The Last of the Peshwas

A Tale of the Third Maratha War

MICHAEL MACMILLAN

ILLUSTRATED BY PAUL HARDY

GYAN

Published by

GYAN

Gyan Publishing House
5, Ansari Road
Daryaganj, New Delhi-110002
Phone: 011-47034999, 9811692060
E-mail: books@gyanbooks.com

Distribution Network
gyanbooks.com
India, USA, Canada, UK, Australia, France

ISBN : 978-81-212-9194-1 (PB)
First Published, 1907

2nd Impression 2023

Printed at: Gyan Press, Delhi.

The Last of the Peshwas
Author: MICHAEL MACMILLAN

"THE SHOCK DROVE HIS HORSE BACK ON ITS HAUNCHES"

The Last of the Peshwas

A Tale of the Third Maratha War

BY

MICHAEL MACMILLAN

Author of "Tales of Indian Chivalry" "In Wild Maratha Battle" "The Princess of Balkh"

ILLUSTRATED BY PAUL HARDY

BLACKIE AND SON LIMITED

LONDON GLASGOW DUBLIN BOMBAY

1907

TO THE MEMORY OF

J. D.

THE EXILE'S DREAM

Our ship, as swift as the lightning flash,
Clove with her prow the waves that dash
Tumultuously with thunderous roar
At midnight on an Indian shore,
And those whereunder buried lie
Busiris' Memphian chivalry.
Then o'er the midland wavelets blue
To Calpe's cannoned steep we flew,
And in a moment southward far
St. Vincent left and Trafalgar.
Ah! joy to feel the northern blast
That on our brows the snowflake cast,
Till loomed a land of hodden gray
Half-hidden by the Atlantic spray,
Behind whose misty canopy
Was heard the peewit's eerie cry.
What magic ship thus bore my soul
Like flash of lightning to her goal
Across the seas that lay between?
A dream of days that once had been.
And what that land of hodden gray?
The bonnie hills of Galloway,
On which my steps no more may stray,
For ever and aye.

CONTENTS

ILLUSTRATIONS

THE
LAST OF THE PESHWAS

CHAPTER I

IN THE VALLEY OF THE FLEET

ONE of the most beautiful valleys in Scotland is that formed by the River Fleet, as it flows from the Highlands of Galloway to the little bay that bears its name. Nowhere in the world is there a finer contrast between the barren grandeur of the granite mountains and the fertile beauty of the valley watered by the river, when at last, after descending one cataract after another, it approaches within two or three miles of the sea, and flows along in a more level stream. Nowhere in the world can be found a richer profusion of all manner of wild flowers than there adorns the river-banks and meadows. The surrounding mountains are purple with heather, and the moorland breezes waft fresh perfumes from beds of bog myrtle, while the air of the valley is fragrant through the summer months and the shortening days of early autumn with the scent of honeysuckle, wild thyme, clover, and meadow-sweet. All the beauty of the scene may be taken in at a glance from the summit of the wooded hill of Castramont, which derives its name either from an ancient British camp that was once pitched on the hill, or from an old Celtic word meaning a forest of elder-trees.

The name Castramont was also given to a small mansion not far from Castramont Hill. My father, who succeeded to the house and estate seventy years ago, belonged to the old Galloway family of MacCulloch. His small property included the wood between the house and Castramont Hill, as well as a few farms on the left bank of the river. Half a mile from the house, by crossing a ford, you would come to the old castle of Rusko, where dwelt another laird, Sir John Hannay, who was master of a larger property, stretching for two or three miles along the right bank of the river to the little country town of Gatehouse-on-Fleet, built where the fresh water of the river first mingles with the tide of the sea and flows into Fleet Bay.

Sir John's family consisted of a son and a daughter, but at the time when my story begins the son was no longer in the castle of Rusko. Much against his father's will, he had gone into the army, and about a year before the commencement of my story had sailed with his regiment, the 18th Hussars, to India. He had distinguished himself in active service against the Pindarries, whose ruffian bands were then devastating India. Then the startling intelligence came that John Hannay had mysteriously disappeared. During a short period of leave he had gone into the Maratha country near Mahableshwar to hunt tigers and panthers. One day he left his tent quite alone, gun in hand, and never returned. The strictest search revealed no sign that gave a clue to the mystery of his disappearance. He might have been killed and devoured by a tiger, or murdered by robbers, or perhaps he had been made prisoner and was languishing in one of the many fortresses with which the Maratha country is studded, for, although the Marathas were nominally at peace with us, it was well known that their monarch, the Peshwa, and many of his nobles, were bitterly hostile. His fate was left in painful uncertainty that was evidently bringing down the gray hairs of his father in sorrow to the ground, and extinguished the gaiety that had once been not the least attractive of the charms of his only sister, Alice.

At this time my father was still strong and active, although he was approaching his fiftieth year. My mother was about five years younger. She was still very beautiful—more beautiful, perhaps, than she had been in the first bloom of youth—for her delicate features had become still more refined by years of happy life divided between her duties as the mistress of the house and the cultivation of the artistic and intellectual tastes that she had inherited from her father. With her skilful paint-brush she reproduced on the canvas the many picturesque scenes that beautify the valley of the Fleet, and in the cold winter months delighted to read the poetry of France, Italy, and her own country. It was my great good fortune that I heartily sympathized with her literary tastes and shared her artistic susceptibility. From childhood it was my chief delight to sit by her as she transferred to her glowing canvas the beauties of wood, moorland, and river-bank, or to hear her read aloud her favourite poems, as I sat on the floor with my head leaning against her knee. When I was old enough to learn French and Italian, she found in me an eager pupil in these languages. Nor was the knowledge of the dead languages of Greece and Rome denied me. Every day, in summer or in winter, in sunshine or in storm, I rode over to Gatehouse to study theology and the ancient classics under the guidance of the old minister of Girthon parish, who had gained high honours as a scholar at Edinburgh University. At first my brother rode with me to the manse to share in the benefits of old Mr. M'Gill's teaching. But it very soon became apparent that he had no taste for literary study. Indeed he was entirely his father's son, and never cared to read a book unless it treated of agriculture or the diseases of horses, cattle, and pigs, and the means of curing them. His mind was severely practical, and his chief talent was an intuitive knowledge of husbandry, which made him an invaluable assistant to my father in the management of the small estate and home farm. This was as it should be. He, as the eldest son, was to succeed my father as laird of Castramont, while my love of books naturally pointed to the conclusion that I was born to be a minister, and, as my old nurse expressed it, to "wag my pow in a pu'pit".

As was to be expected, there was close intimacy between the two lairds and their respective families. In childhood we played together, and were continually exchanging visits or going in company to gather wild flowers, blackberries, or hazel-nuts. As we grew up to manhood or womanhood, we kept up, in spite of transitory quarrels, the old intimacy, and called each other by our Christian names, like brothers and sisters. Alice Hannay, being the one girl in the company, was in some danger of being spoiled. Some of the quarrels to which I have alluded arose from the keen competition among us as to who should do most for her. If she expressed a wish for a bunch of the auspicious but rare white heather, each of us would be ready to clamber up the highest mountains or scour the wild moorland round Loch Skerrow in the hope of gratifying her wish. In our long rambles through field, forest, or moorland we were all equally eager to give her a helping hand when she had to get over the high walls of loose stones by which one sheep-walk in

Galloway is separated from another. Not that she really needed much help, for, from constantly being in the company of boys in the open air, she was almost as active and strong as the best of us, and it would have been a very high and shaky dyke that she would not have been able to surmount unaided, had she been inclined to do so.

Although my brother and I were devoted to Alice, it was in the way of friendship, not of love. At least so we thought, for neither of us knew the real state of our feelings until Tom and I had reached respectively the ages of twenty and eighteen. At this time the news came from India of the mysterious disappearance of John Hannay, and almost every day we would go over to express our sympathy with Alice and her father, and ask if any better news had come from India.

CHAPTER II

JEALOUSY AWAKES LOVE

ON one of those visits we found Alice in the garden in front of the house, but not alone. She was walking up and down in earnest conversation with a young man, elegantly dressed in irreproachable attire, such as no Galloway or even Edinburgh tailor could have fashioned. His coat was pinched in at the waist in a way that gave plain evidence of the presence of corsets. His tight-fitting pantaloons showed off to advantage his well-shaped legs. Three or four heavy seals dangled from his waist. A ruffle of the finest cambric, edged with lace, protruded from under his chin, which was supported by a black stock, and a high collar rose to his ears. As he walked he tapped his feet ever and anon with a thin ebony walking-stick. His face was regular in feature, but effeminate, and the light-brown hair over his forehead appeared to have been curled by artificial means. Immediately we

B 592

"SHE WAS WALKING UP AND DOWN IN EARNEST CONVERSATION WITH A YOUNG MAN"

set eyes upon him we felt an instinctive impulse of hatred and jealousy, and thus was revealed to us the love of which we had till then been unconscious. Alice introduced him to us as Captain Moore of the 18th Hussars, who had recently returned with his regiment from India. He greeted us with an easy well-bred smile, which, I fear, neither of us had the good manners to return. We did not care, before a stranger, to speak to Alice of her brother's loss, and after answering curtly one or two enquiries that Captain Moore put to us about the shooting and fishing in the neighbourhood, we entered the castle to see Sir John, and after a short conversation about the terrible misfortune that had befallen him, left Rusko without even bidding Alice farewell.

As we walked gloomily back together across the ford to Castramont, my brother said to me:

"Can you tell me why it is, Aleck, that I feel as though I should like to fight that English dandy and spoil his beauty."

"The reason," I replied, "must be that you are in love with Alice and madly jealous. Strange to say, my feelings are just the same.

Would that we lived in the good old times, that I might challenge him to meet me in the lists, breast to breast and lance to lance!"

"For me," replied Tom, "I should just as willingly meet him face to face and fist to fist, and give him a bluidy nose or a black eye. But you are always in imagination like one of the heroes of your poetry books, and must be trying to live the life of a knight-errant of romance in this workaday world. Take care you don't come to grief tilting at windmills, like that madman in the Spanish book you and mother are so fond of reading."

Our tempers were not improved when we reached Castramont, and our old nurse Susan Burns, who had now become housekeeper, asked us if we had seen Miss Alice's fine English cousin, who had come all the way from London town to marry her and succeed her father as laird of Rusko when the old man died.

That night, for the first time in my life, I enjoyed little sleep. The consciousness of a deep passion, and despair of my love ever being returned, kept my brain in a wild state of excitement. Such sleep as came to me was disturbed by a dream that recurred again and again. I seemed to be wandering through Castramont wood in the severe silence of a moonless night. By the dim light of the stars, shining through the branches of the trees, I followed the shadowy figure of a woman robed in white who ever eluded my pursuit. Although I never saw her face, I knew in my soul that it was Alice who fled before me. Then I would find myself on the top of Castramont Hill, and its wooded height changed into a strong fortress defended by great precipices of rock and mighty masonry. Over the ramparts peered "dark faces with white silken turbans wreathed", like the faces of those whom Milton saw, in imagination, proceeding along the Appian Road to offer the tribute of the East to Imperial Cæsar. Then a white face showed itself on the topmost turret, with the well-known features of Alice's brother, John. He stretched out his hands to me in an attitude of supplication, and besought me to enter in and free him from imprisonment. But when I approached the great gate of the fortress, and hammered at it with a battle-axe that somehow was in my hand, I would awake and restlessly toss on my couch till sleep again overcame me and I once more began to thread the labyrinth of the wood in vain pursuit of the shadowy figure, and once more found myself under the walls of the great fortress. Such was the dream that went on repeating itself in my brain through the night like a recurring decimal, until it was driven away by the bright arrows of the dawn.

CHAPTER III

ON THE WHITE TAP OF CULREOCH

BEFORE sunrise I was up and dressed, determined to conquer by hard physical exercise the mental trouble that oppressed me. My new *rôle* of disappointed lover, in spite of a certain amount of pain and grief, was not without its attractions. Was I not thereby raised to the level of Petrarch, Shakespeare, and a host of other poets, who had turned their disappointments into melodious strains of lyric poetry! Old Susan, who, for the practical purpose of waking up the maids, was up as early as I was, met me on the stairs, and urged me to take a bite of food before starting out so early in the morning. But, not to be behind the lovers of romance whose conduct I was emulating, I replied in tragic tones that I could not eat, and, to her great distress, hurried out of the house without taking anything to stay my stomach till my return.

It would have suited my romantic mood if I could have mounted my coal-black or milk-white steed and galloped him in furious guise along the road to Gatehouse. Unfortunately the horse that I usually rode, which happened to be of a dull nondescript colour, such as is never celebrated in poetry, was required to do some hard work on the home farm that day, so I had to leave him in the stable and go out on foot. Without definite intention I turned my steps towards the moorland. I did not much care where I went, as long as I could emulate the example of Bellerophon, who, when he thought himself hated by all the gods, went wandering along the Aleian plain, eating his soul and avoiding the path of men. Presently before me towered the White Tap of Culreoch, the highest mountain in the immediate neighbourhood. Putting a "stout heart to a stey brae", I clambered up the bed of the mountain torrent that flows down the mountain-side. Before I was half-way up, the clouds began to gather round me, and when I sat down on the cairn at the top of the mountain I was enveloped in a thick mist that prevented me from seeing far in front of me. The spot was not devoid of poetical associations. It was not far from here that Burns, on his way from Gatehouse to Castle-Douglas, in a tremendous storm of thunder and lightning, composed the greatest of Scottish war lyrics, a poem that thrills through the heart of every true-born Scotchman in whatever part of the world it is heard. In the surrounding moorland the heather had often been dyed with the blood of those who "raised the psalm to wintry skies", and were surprised at their worship by Grierson of Lag, or Claverhouse. Thus, even if I had not been at once exalted and depressed by the deep feelings that accompany the revelation of first love, the position I occupied was one that naturally inspired poetic moralizing.

Seated on the cairn in the thickening mist, I gave the rein to my gloomy thoughts, and soon succeeded in convincing myself that, though I was young and strong and not oppressed by poverty or by the death of any of those near and dear to me, life was not worth living. I succeeded in confirming myself in this irrational conclusion by concentrating my attention on my deep love and the assumed hopelessness of my passion being ever returned. My discovery that I was deeply in love had been due to the sudden appearance of a rival who had every advantage over me, and was, I felt sure, bound to be successful. For how could such a country-bred boy as I was hope to compete in a lady's eye with a fashionable beau who was accomplished in all the airs and graces of London society? He was, as I had heard, a fine player on the violin and a fine dancer. He had also more solid recommendations. He had not only been to India and the continent of Europe, but had also borne himself well as an officer in a distinguished cavalry regiment. It was no consolation for me to know that my brother was in the same position as myself. I loved him too well to be glad that he should be suffering what I suffered. And if by any chance Captain Moore had not made a conquest of Alice's heart, then my brother Tom would be, instead of him, my successful rival. For I recognized clearly his many excellent qualities, and knew that in goodness and firmness of character he was my superior. Also, as the heir to my father's small estate, he would assuredly be preferred as a suitor, by Alice's father at any rate, to his younger brother. So my thoughts grew darker and darker as the mist gradually thickened round the cairn on which I was sitting.

The mist had now become so thick that it was dangerous to attempt to descend. However, I presently grew tired of sitting still, and determined to make the attempt. I started at a good pace, and had walked at a smart pace for fifteen or twenty minutes, when a cairn of stones suddenly loomed through the mist. At this moment it struck me that the wind had changed, and, to my surprise, blew upon me from the opposite direction to that from which it had blown when I first left the top of the mountain. On examining the cairn I soon found the explanation of the change in the direction of the wind. The cairn turned out to be the very same heap of stones which I had left twenty minutes before! Whether my right leg had outwalked my left, or I had unconsciously edged away from the descent for fear of falling over a precipice, the result was that, for want of guidance from surrounding objects, my steps had led me round in a circle to the exact spot from which I had started.

One satisfactory result of this strange experience was that it restored me to a true estimate of the value of life. The dangerous position in which I now found myself convinced me that, after all, even for a hopeless lover, life was well worth living. Somehow or other the possibility of stepping suddenly over a precipice, from time into eternity, demonstrates more clearly than the best-reasoned discourses of optimistic philosophers the desirability of life. Certainly on this occasion I did not take the opportunity of going straight over the precipice, but, on the contrary, with due caution started once more on my downward path, this time taking care to keep the wind blowing on my right cheek, lest I should again inadvertently walk in a circle. By means of this precaution I succeeded in getting down the mountain-side till I struck the course of the stream that I had followed in the beginning of my ascent of the mountain. Presently the mist began to get thinner, and before I reached the junction of the stream with the River Fleet nothing was left of it except the drops of moisture, that sparkled in the sunlight like diamonds, on the trees, the heather, and the grass.

CHAPTER IV

WITH ALICE IN THE FAIRY GLEN

ABOUT half a mile above the spot where it flows into the River Fleet, the mountain torrent rushes over a granite ledge into a deep pool fifty feet below. The pool and its surroundings were so lovely that it was one of our favourite haunts, and we had given it the name of the Fairy Glen. The rocks on either side of the cascade are overshadowed by hazel, alder, birch, and rowan trees, and adorned with soft green moss, ferns, and many flowers, from the homely ragged-robin to the stately grass of Parnassus. The pure water of the pool is so pellucid that you can see at its bottom clearly the shape and colour of every pebble, except when the torrent is swollen by rain and covers it with white foam. Often had my brother and I, when heated by the summer sun, enjoyed the refreshing coolness of its waters, and let the cascade flow like a natural shower-bath over our heads and shoulders, and always the pleasure of the bathe was enhanced by the fairy-like beauty of the scene.

As I glanced in passing at this beautiful spot, what was my surprise to see a lady sitting on a stone close to the margin of the pool, and gazing into its watery depth! It was Alice, and her gray eyes were full of tears. Beside her lay unread a volume of the latest romance of the Great Unknown. She turned her head at my approach, and greeted me with a wan smile, like a gleam of sunlight in a wintry sky.

"Well, Aleck," she said, "where have you been so early in the morning? But perhaps you won't speak to me. Yesterday you and Tom did not seem to have much to say to me."

"You had a handsome cavalier by your side," I replied, "who was more fit to talk to such a fine lady as you than two plain Galloway lads like me and my brother. We saw you were having a very interesting conversation, and did not venture to interrupt it."

My conscience smote me as I uttered this unfeeling taunt to one whom I loved above all the rest of the world, and that at a time when her eyes were suffused with tears. The truth is, that just before arriving at the waterfall I had changed my mood, and was steeling my mind against the pangs of despised love by humming to myself Wither's song:

> "Shall I, wasting in despair,
> Die because a woman's fair?
> What care I how fair she be
> If she be not fair to me!"

With these words on my lips it was not easy for me to drop down immediately from the affected dignity of a lover scorned. But it was only a transitory caprice of school-boy petulance. When Alice, by dropping a silent tear, showed me how hurt she was by my rudeness, I was disarmed in a moment, and before I well knew what I was doing I found myself kneeling down to kiss her hand, and imploring her forgiveness if I had offended her. If she had been angry, she was easily appeased.

"Do not be vexed, Aleck dear," she said. "You did not mean to be unkind. Of course you did not quite mean what you said. You know how fond I am of you and Tom, and that the finest courtier from St. James's Palace could never for a moment be preferred to you two, who are now, alas! the only brothers I have left."

It can be easily imagined how these kind and gentle words heaped coals of fire on my head. I besought her to tell me what I could do to atone for my rudeness.

"Well," she replied, "you must first tell me where you have been, and why you look so pale and tired, just as if you had spent the whole night wandering among those misty mountains."

I answered, with a smile, that she had nearly guessed the truth, and told her of my sleepless night, my long morning walk, and how the mist had caught me on the White Tap of Culreoch. Her kind heart made her shudder at the danger I had undergone.

"You must be not only tired but also hungry," she said. "What did you have to eat before you started on your long walk?"

When I confessed how, in spite of Susan Burns's advice, I had taken nothing, she started up and looked quite serious.

"You foolish boy!" she exclaimed; "how could you be so foolish and naughty as to disobey your good old nurse? Go home immediately to your breakfast. I will accompany you, and on the way you shall tell me what prevented you from sleeping and prompted you to act so very, very foolishly."

Then, as we walked homeward through the greenwood, I opened my heart to her and told my simple tale of love and jealousy.

"I have now," I said in conclusion, "made my confession of love. If I live to the age of a hundred I can love no one but you alone. But I am conscious of my own unworthiness. You have only to tell me that you prefer your fine London cousin, or my true-hearted brother, who is a far better man than I can ever hope to be, and I will go to India or some other distant part of the world. For you would not ask me to stay here and see you the bride of another."

Alice hastened to assure me that she had not lost her heart to her cousin, to my brother, or to anyone else.

"But," she added, "how could I think of love when my dear brother is dead or a captive in a distant land? What else was I talking about so earnestly to Captain Moore but my brother's fate? There is room in my heart and mind for no other thought at present.

The only thing that could add to my unhappiness was that you or Tom should be unkind to me."

The mild reproach came home to me. How could I have had the heart to wound with my foolish jealousy a sister mourning for a lost brother, who was also my own bosom friend! I was eager to make amends. The knights of old showed their devotion to their lady-loves by undertaking some perilous adventure. Was there not such an adventure open to me now if I would only seize the opportunity! So I exclaimed passionately:

"If I may not speak of love to you now, let me go and look for your lost brother. Should it be my good fortune to find him and restore him to his home, might I then have hope of winning your hand?"

"No," she said; "I fear from what Captain Moore told me that my brother must be no more, and if you go to that terrible country, I might lose in you another brother."

But when I told her my dream, she was of a different mind. She was even more disposed than myself to put faith in dreams and omens, and what I had told her revived her hopes of seeing her brother again.

"This dream," she said, "may have been sent by a Higher Power to call you to the task of delivering my brother from captivity. Achieve this, and you need not fear that I will refuse you my hand, if such a slight prize would be worthy the acceptance of a knight who performs such a noble deed."

We then parted at the gate of Castramont, and I entered the house full of the gladness of hope and of the high thoughts inspired by the enterprise I had undertaken. Old Susan, in her snow-white mutch, greeted me at the door with words of sympathy.

"My puir bairn," she exclaimed, "ye maun be starvin' o' hunger, and, my certes, ye're lookin' gey an' white! Whaur hae ye been sae lang wi'oot takin' bite or sup? Come awa' in. They're a' at their breakfast. But ye maun tidy yersel' a bit first, for Sir John and the English captain and twa or three ithers hae looked in tae tak' breakfast wi' yer faither and mither."

What breakfasts these were in Galloway, and what appetites we had to do justice to them! There were oat-cakes, soda and potato scones, kippered salmon, pig's cheek, trout caught that morning in the Fleet by my brother Tom, bacon and eggs, grouse, and, horrible feast for an enamoured swain, "bluid puddens" black and white. Now that I am getting on in years, and long residence in India has somewhat impaired my appetite, I often think with wonder on such a meal as I then enjoyed, and in my recollections of Galloway it must be confessed that pleasant memories of those mighty breakfasts mingle in ill-assorted union with recollections of the beautiful scenery of lake, river, and mountain. He was a wise man who said that, if he had his choice, he would breakfast in Scotland, lunch in England, and dine in France.

CHAPTER V

I BECOME A CADET IN THE OLD TOUGHS

AFTER the breakfast recorded at the end of the previous chapter, I invited Captain Moore out to have a smoke with me in the garden. On finding that he was not to be regarded as a successful rival, I had entirely got over my aversion to him, and found him to be a most agreeable companion, although he seemed somewhat affected in his manners and language. But this was perhaps because I had never lived in the fashionable world of London.

We sat down together in the garden under the shade of the great fir-tree, which is, I am convinced, one of the tallest trees in Scotland. He refused to smoke with me, but solaced himself with frequent pinches of snuff out of a beautiful little snuff-box of blue Sèvres porcelain. When I told him that I was going out to Bombay to look for Alice's lost brother, he gave me much information about Bombay and

Western India, which he described as one of the most dismal places in the world.

"Englishmen," he said, "cannot live long in Bombay. They have an old saying there that two monsoons are the life of a man, and I do not think it is far from the truth. Nor is life in Bombay worth living. The place is deadly dull, and the climate gradually destroys the energy and vital strength."

I called his attention to the instance of my uncle, who had lived in Bombay for many years, and, as far as I knew, enjoyed good health.

"Yes," he said, "I knew the old man a little. He lived like a Brahmin, and so managed to survive. But what is the good of living if you give up wine and every other enjoyment?"

"Et propter vitam vivendi perdere causas," I replied, perhaps a little too eager to display my erudition.

He did not, however, show any appreciation of my apposite quotation, but went on to do his best to dissuade me from my enterprise by urging upon me the reason why there was little hope of my being successful.

"If John Hannay," he said, "had been

captured by the Pindarries or Marathas, they would either have killed him at once or kept him alive for the sake of a ransom or exchange of prisoners. I cannot imagine why they should take the trouble to keep a captive alive in a secret prison. If I thought this likely, I should myself go back to India on the chance of finding him. Perhaps, if I brought back her brother, the fair Alice might look with kinder eyes on one who is eager to be her slave."

He was shrewd enough to infer something of the state of my feelings from the shade of annoyance that passed over my countenance as he made this reference to Alice. So he frankly added:

"Perhaps you, too, are in love with my fair cousin. Well, I will not challenge you to deadly combat on that account. She is, if you will allow me to say so, a very beautiful girl, all the more so because of the pale cast of thought that is due to mourning over the loss of her brother. But there are many other fair girls in the world, who may smile more kindly upon me, and, as my favourite poet says: 'I ne'er saw beauty in an eye that would not sweetly smile on mine'."

After this he gave me information as to the way in which a commission in the Indian army could best be got in those days, for I could not ask my father to bear the expense of my travelling to India. On the other hand, I had long cherished an ambition to serve my country and win my way to distinction by military service in India. Elphinstone and Malcolm were still in the prime of life, and had made themselves great names in the civil and military service in the Bombay Presidency. Why should not another young Scotchman follow them to the East and emulate their great example? The captain told me that cadetships in the Indian army could be obtained through influence with the East India Company, and that he would willingly move his friends there in my behalf. I thanked him for his kindness, but knew I should not need his help, as my uncle, David MacCulloch, who was a merchant in Bombay, was a great power in Leadenhall Street.

David MacCulloch had the reputation of being as eccentric as he was rich. He went out to Bombay at a very early age to make his way in the world as a merchant. When my grandfather died, my uncle had already laid the foundations of a great fortune, and refused to succeed to the small estate of Castramont, although he was the eldest son. He had often since then expressed his readiness to take me out and give me a desk in his office; but I had no taste for business, and was unwilling to accept the offer. Now, however, I determined to use his influence in Leadenhall Street to procure me a cadetship in the Indian army.

My father and mother were induced to give their sanction to my project, although it was a sad grief to the latter to think of her son going so far away from home. I had never before been at a greater distance from Castramont than Edinburgh. Even a journey to London was a great undertaking for such a homebred youth as I was, and now I was about to start for the Indies. However, I must push on with my story. I need not dwell on the sad hour of my parting with my parents, my brother, and Alice, nor attempt to describe the feelings with which, as my horse bore me along the road to Gatehouse, I took my last fond look at the top of the great fir-tree that towered above Castramont garden. Suffice it to say that from Gatehouse I rode on to Kirkcudbright, whence I crossed in a smack to Liverpool. From Liverpool the coach bore me swiftly to London, and I lost no time in calling on Mr. Leslie, my uncle's partner in London.

Mr. Leslie's reception of me gave me a foretaste of Anglo-Indian hospitality. He insisted on my removing immediately, with all my bag and baggage, to his house in Bloomsbury from the hotel to which I had gone. He was delighted to do all in his power for the nephew of his friend, David MacCulloch, and this proved to be more than an empty expression of good-will. Only a few days after my arrival in London I was summoned to appear before the Court of Directors. At the India Office I was informed that my name had been duly entered for a cadetship in the Bombay European Regiment, popularly known as the Old Toughs, and I took the oath of allegiance. As war was going on against the Pindarries in Western India, and it was expected that we should soon also be at open war with the Marathas, I was embarked with as little delay as possible, with a dozen other cadets and a regiment of European infantry, on the troopship *Ajax*, commanded by Captain Dixon.

The voyage to Bombay was very prosperous and rapid. We left London in the end of May, and reached our destination on the 3rd of October. However, even at its best, in those days a voyage to India in a troopship was far from agreeable. The drinking-water was bad, the biscuits were mouldy, and it was only the freshness of the sea-breezes that enabled us to find an appetite for the continually reiterated salt junk. In accordance with Mr. Leslie's advice I occupied myself on board by studying Marathi, the language of the part of India in which I was likely to be engaged in warlike campaigns and in the search for Alice's brother. Having a natural aptitude for picking up languages, I made rapid progress by dint of studying Carey's Grammar and Dictionary. I also took lessons from Captain Dixon's native servant, Haibati, who spoke the Maratha language. At last the voyage was completed, and, full of hope, I stepped ashore on the island of Bombay in the last week of October, in the memorable year 1817.

CHAPTER VI

A CANARY'S OBSEQUIES

IT was early morning when I landed in Bombay. The sun was rising over the Maratha hills on the other side of the harbour, and illuminating Bombay Castle and the buildings collected round it in the Fort or European business portion of the island, which is so called because it is, or I should rather say was, surrounded by a high wall. Great changes have taken place in Bombay during the half-century that has elapsed since the time of which I am writing. The walls of the fort, useless as a defence against modern artillery, have all been pulled down, so as not only to economize space, but also to allow the sea-breeze to blow more freely through the streets and houses. Many fine buildings have been erected, so that the lines that Heber wrote long ago:

> "Thy towers, Bombay, gleam fair, they say,
> Across the dark blue sea,"

were truer as a prophecy than as a description of the actual appearance of the city at the time when they were written. When I landed there, the only tower visible was that of St. Thomas's Cathedral, towards which I walked across Bombay Green on my way to my uncle's house.

In the middle of the Green I met a rather strange figure, clad in white nankin coat and trousers, and with a native turban on his head. He was tall and thin, and had a large, beaked nose and prominent cheek-bones. In his right hand he held a thick cane with a silver top, and in his left he carried with tender care a little box of carved sandal-wood. The man whom I had engaged to guide me through Bombay whispered in my ear: "That is MacCulloch Sahib."

I immediately went over to greet him, and introduced myself as his nephew. He transferred his silver-topped cane to a servant who was attending him, and, thus disencumbered, shook hands with me most heartily, exclaiming:

"So you are the birkie that wadna be content to come and sit on a high stule in my office, and be a rich merchant and the heir to a' the gowd I hae pit thegither in the land o' the heathen! Ye maun needs be a sodger, and gang and get yer throat cut, or a bullet shot through whar yer harns suld be, by thae Marathas. Weel, weel! Gang yer ain gait. But dinna blame me gin ye fare nae better than puir John Hannay, that's either deid or in a dungeon on ane o' yon hills."

As he spoke, he pointed across the harbour to the mountains, many of whose tops were crowned with Maratha fortresses.

"Ye hae met me," he added, "at a sad moment. I hae juist come oot tae bury my dearest freen', and his corp is noo lyin' in this wee box."

I asked whether his lost friend was a Hindu, for I knew that the Hindus burned their dead, and, in my ignorance of Hindu manners and customs, thought that the ashes of some cremated native of the country might be enclosed in the sandal-wood box.

"Na, na," he explained; "my freen' was no a man but a bird—a wee bit canary, that woke me ilka mornin' wi' his sweet singin', and wad feed oot o' my hand."

His feelings seemed so deeply moved by his bereavement that I did not venture to speak of any other subject until the obsequies of the canary were completed. His servant dug a grave for it under a banyan-tree, and as he replaced the earth over the box, my uncle gazed fixedly on the ground.

"Maybe that wee bird will be the first to welcome me into Paradise," he said, and then, with a sad countenance, he led me to his house.

CHAPTER VII

MY UNCLE IN BOMBAY

UNLIKE many of the English merchants in Bombay, who had their private houses in the fashionable suburb of Mazagon, or at a distance of four miles from the Fort, my uncle lived above his office, in rooms five stories high, that commanded a wide prospect across the harbour on one side, and on the other side over Back Bay to Malabar Hill. Their height opened them to the west wind, which blew over the lower roofs of the neighbouring buildings. Nevertheless, at breakfast we were further cooled by the artificial breeze of the punkah, a huge fan hanging from the roof, and made to swing over our heads by the efforts of one of my uncle's many servants. The other novelties at the breakfast were plantains (red and white) and a flat fish called the pomphlet, which Bombay gourmands extol as superior to the English sole, the Scotch salmon, and all other fish in the world. Another excellent dish was a curry composed of prawns, which in Bombay are large and plentiful.

After breakfast a hubble-bubble was brought in by a servant, whose chief office was to attend to this gigantic species of pipe or smoking-machine, so called because of the sound made by the smoke passing through a receptacle containing water. I was provided with delicious cheroots from Southern India. As we smoked, my uncle forgot, or pretended out of politeness to forget, his dead pet, and we had a long talk about public and private affairs, from which I derived much valuable information.

All the mainland immediately round Bombay, and as far as the centre of India, was seething with anarchy, and in a state of actual or imminent civil war. The plundering armies of the fierce Pindarries had for many years laid waste great tracts of India, and oppressed rich and poor with horrible cruelty—torturing the rich to extort money from them, and wantonly ill-treating the poor because they had no money to give. To suppress them, Lord Hastings had taken the field with a great army, over a hundred thousand strong, supported by the nominal alliance of the

Peshwa and the Marathas. But the Marathas were divided among themselves, and at heart more disposed to go to war with the British than to join heartily in the operations against the Pindarries. Above all, the Peshwa Baji Rao II, who, in his capital city of Poona, claimed sovereignty over all the Marathas, was very hostile to the British. His creature, Trimbakji Danglia, one of the cruellest and most unscrupulous men that ever lived, had, with the Peshwa's connivance, murdered Gangadhar Shastri, a learned Brahmin, who had gone to the Peshwa's court under British protection. The Peshwa had in May been compelled to accept a treaty which, if carried out, would make him a dependant of the British Indian Empire; but it was well known that he was eager to take the first opportunity of rebelling, and employing against the British the troops he had raised ostensibly to take part in the war against the Pindarries.

Having finished his account of the state of public affairs, my uncle proceeded next to discuss the private object which had led me to India. He could not throw any light on the mystery of John Hannay's disappearance.

"I kent the lad weel," he said, "and liked

him weel. But he wasna canny, and was ower free wi' his money, and was ower thick wi' that braw ne'er-do-weel cousin o' his. Did ye ever meet wi' Captain Moore?" he asked.

I told him how much I had seen of Captain Moore, and added that we had all been delighted with him.

"Ay," he said, "he's gey fair spoken, and kens weel the best way to get roon' them he wants to be freen's wi', abune a', rich young men that he wants to fleece at the deil's buiks, or billiards, or ony ither kind o' gambling."

"Was he a gambler?" I asked in surprise.

"Ay; he wad play for money a' the nicht through, till the birds began to sing. When he was at Poona, they say he used to play cards wi' the Peshwa and his nobles, and he maun hae made a gey hantle o' siller by his skill. My certes! he couldna hae kept a' the fine horses and machines that he had in his bungalow on his captain's pay; and I ken weel that he got nae mair than a hundred pounds a year frae his freen's in England, for a' the siller that cam' to him frae London passed through my hands. But I canna bandy ony mair words wi' ye the noo. I maun gang to my office and see what advices hae come to me by your ship frae England and Scotland. Report yer arrival to the general, and gang roon' the toon and see a' that's to be seen, for I'm thinking ye'll sune hae to gang to Poona to fecht thae Maratha deevils that disturb the peace o' the country, and interfere wi' honest trade."

My uncle was one of a not uncommon class of Scotchmen, who show their devotion to their native land in every way except by living in it. Although he had been absent from Scotland for twenty years, he still affected to speak the broadest Scotch. He was a regular attendant at the Scottish Kirk, and, although economical in his private expenditure, liberally supported Scotch charities at home and in India. His rooms were adorned with pictures of Scottish scenery, among which I particularly noticed some beautiful coloured engravings of Cardoness Castle, Gatehouse, Creetown, Wigtown, and other familiar Galloway localities by Daniel. I saw also framed, in a prominent position on the wall of his dining-room, an autograph letter of Burns, whose friendship with his father at Dumfries[1] was a great source of pride to him. He was also proud of his con-

[1] See Appendix, note 1.

nection with Scott, whose brother had married his aunt. His copy of the Kilmarnock edition of Burns's works was well-worn with constant reading. Indeed, I never saw him with any other book in his hands except Burns, the Bible, and the poems and novels of Scott. He had taught his cook to make oatmeal porridge and oat-cake, which still were the principal elements in his diet, as they had been when he was a little boy running wild, and often barefooted, in the valley of Fleet. He was not very sociable with his fellowmen, even with those of his own nationality, except at the great dinners celebrated in Bombay on St. Andrew's Day, when he revelled in the whisky and haggis and songs that on that famous anniversary unite the souls of Scotchmen in amity all over the world.

However, I at any rate received from him a most genial welcome, especially at dinner, when his heart was warmed with rather copious potations of the national drink. He gave me good practical advice against extravagance and falling into debt, but at the same time besought me, if I ever should be in want of money, to apply to him before having recourse to native money-lenders.

On this particular occasion I was not able to make a long stay at my uncle's. Early next morning an urgent despatch came to Bombay from Mr. Mountstuart Elphinstone, the British resident at the Peshwa's court in Poona, requesting that the Company's European regiment in Bombay, the regiment in which I had obtained a cadetship, should join him as fast as possible without regard to anything but the health of the men. As the critical state of affairs at Poona was well known in Bombay, Major Wilson, the officer in command of the regiment, had long been in hourly expectation of such an order, and was ready to march immediately.

My uncle gave me a letter of introduction to Hari Rao, an influential native banker in Poona, who would supply me with any money I wanted, and might help me in other ways. He bade me a kindly farewell, and gave me, as a parting gift, a chain-mail tunic of Oriental workmanship, which was a wonderful combination of lightness and strength. It could be worn under my military tunic, and would, he said, prove impervious to lance or sword.

CHAPTER VIII

I VISIT A HINDU BANKER

ON the following morning we crossed the harbour in large boats to Panwell. On first entering Maratha territory I observed with interest the changes that marked the difference between British and native rule. The fort of Bellapoor, intended to defend the town, was in a dilapidated state. The workmen in the town and in the country kept sword and spear constantly at hand, ready for a sudden attack, and had their swords girded by their sides, like the Jews when they rebuilt the walls of Jerusalem under the directions of Nehemiah. The people appeared to be well fed and comfortable, which was attributed to the prosperity due to the opportunities they had of obtaining work in Bombay and supplying the city with fish. Their religious or superstitious character was attested by the enormous size of their principal pagoda. The surface of the tank near the temple was covered with the great blossoms of the pink lotus, a flower which resembles the English water-lily except in colour.

From Panwell we hurried on by forced marches to Poona, climbing on the way the mountain wall of the Ghauts, at this time of the year clad in verdure, for, though the monsoon rains had now ceased to fall, their effects remained in the green grass and the many torrents that fell in cascades from the mountain heights as we ascended. But in the excitement of our hasty progress we had little leisure to admire the beauties of nature. Our minds were full of anxiety lest the small British force in the centre of the great national capital of the Marathas, and surrounded by many thousands of hostile warriors thirsting for their blood, might be destroyed before our arrival. Early on the morning of the 30th of October we reached Poona, and to our unspeakable relief saw our flag still flying above the British Residency and the cantonments at Garpir.

But we were not a day too soon. The Peshwa's troopers had been making daily demonstrations round the British encampment, and trying to provoke a conflict. On the day before our arrival Bapu Gokhle, the Maratha general, had urged his master to attack the British troops before they were reinforced, but the Peshwa hesitated and lost his opportunity.

Our arrival caused the greatest excitement. The whole city was in a state of most admired and picturesque disorder. Bands of troopers in bright-coloured flowing robes rode through the streets and hustled elephants and gaudy palanquins. Even the ordinary citizens went about armed with sword and shield. Close to our cantonments rode bodies of Maratha horsemen, waving their swords and provoking us with menacing words, to which we were forbidden to reply. It was not by words but by deeds that we were to give our retort to the insults to which we were subjected.

In the afternoon, when I had an hour's remission from my military duties, I made my way to the house of Hari Rao, a rich banker, bearing with me the letter of introduction from my uncle. His wealth gave him great influence at the court of the Peshwa, and he might be able to give me some guidance in my search for traces of John Hannay, who had been last seen and heard of in the neighbourhood of Poona. I therefore determined to seek him out without delay, as it was impossible to know what the morrow might bring forth. Poona was like a powder-magazine with sparks flying about that might at any moment produce an explosion. If war broke out, I might miss my chance of meeting Hari Rao for a long time, or even for ever.

One of the sepoys of the 7th Bombay Native Infantry accompanied me to show me the way to the merchant's house, which was at no great distance from the cantonment. Many a scowl and glance of defiance was hurled at us as we rode along the road; but we were not actually attacked, although provoked almost beyond endurance by the insulting words and looks that we had to hear and see. The door of Hari Rao's house was made of thick teakwood bound with iron, like the gate of a fortress. It was fastened with great bars and chains, and for some time we could not induce those within even to open the small grated window in the upper part of the gate. At last this was opened, and a head appeared behind the grating. We were told in a rough voice that at such a time no admittance could be given to strangers, and ordered to go about our business. My reply was to push in through the grating my uncle's letter of introduction. The man behind the gate took it away, and, returning after ten or fifteen minutes, began to draw back the heavy bar and take off the chains with which the gate was secured inside.

The Indian banking-house which I now entered was very different in appearance from English and Scotch banks. There were no folding-doors silently swinging on their hinges, no solid counters of polished wood with clerks on high stools sitting behind. The clerks were all squatting on cushions on the ground, where they were engaged counting heaps of rupees and entering the results of their calculations in Oriental ledgers bound not in stiff boards but in easily folded leather. When I entered the sanctum of Hari Rao himself, I found myself in a room absolutely devoid of chair and table, and there sat the rich banker, like his clerks, on a cushion. He did not rise to receive me or shake me by the hand or relax his countenance into a smile of welcome, but, remaining seated on his cushion, solemnly touched his forehead with his right hand and motioned me to another cushion on which I could sit facing him. Then, dismissing the attendant who had ushered me into his presence, he bade me declare my business, assuring me with great earnestness that he honoured MacCulloch Sahib as he honoured his gods, and that, since I was his brother's son, he would gladly obey all my orders.

I replied that I had come chiefly to seek for information about the mysterious disappearance of John Hannay, who was my uncle's friend and my own.

"I am afraid," he replied, "that I cannot solve the mystery, but I will truly answer any question on the subject that your honour may be pleased to put to me."

"Did you see John Hannay, when he was in Poona immediately before his disappearance?"

"Yes," replied Hari Rao; "he came to me once to draw money, with another British officer who was well known in Poona and was on intimate terms with many of the Peshwa's nobles."

"Can you tell me the name of that officer?"

"Yes," he replied, "his name was Captain Moore. We natives altered his name into Mor Sahib, because *mor* in our language means a peacock, and he was as vain of his beauty and fine clothes as the peacock is of its gaudy tail. He was a great gambler, but a man of charming manners. He was, indeed, such a favourite with the Peshwa's courtiers that, I am told, he became on that account an object of suspicion to the British Government, and was recalled from Poona to Bombay."

"You only saw my friend on that one occasion?"

"Never before or after," he replied.

"Was he as popular as Captain Moore in the Peshwa's court?"

"No, on the contrary, he was disliked by the Maratha nobles. Those who met him described him as cold and haughty, and contrasted him most unfavourably in this respect with Mor Sahib, whom they all worshipped."

"Did he ever have a quarrel with any of the Maratha nobles?"

"Not that I know. But the duty of friendship and the commands of MacCulloch Sahib compel me to tell you this. Once when I was present at the Peshwa's council, John Hannay's name happened to be mentioned, and the Peshwa, who generally can control his temper and conceal his hatred under a smiling countenance, burst out into a violent execration, and ordered his nobles never to mention that accursed person again in his presence."

"Did this happen before or after John Hannay's disappearance?"

"A few days before," he replied.

"I am told," I went on, "that my friend, when he was last seen in Poona, was about to start on a hunting expedition. Can you tell me if this was the case?"

"This," he answered, "was generally reported, but I have no special information on the subject, except that the shikari[1] who accompanied him said that they were going towards the source of the Kistna."

The mention of the shikari raised my hopes.

"Can I not find that shikari?" I asked.

"I myself caused enquiries to be made for him, but he, too, appears never to have returned to Poona, and I entirely failed to find any trace of him."

"Do you think the sahib and the shikari could both have been killed by a tiger?"

"Such a thing," he said, "is possible, but improbable. It is so improbable that I should be more disposed to think that they were attacked and killed by men. What with the

[1] Shikari = a native huntsman.

Pindarries, and the feuds between the Peshwa and the Maratha nobles, the whole country is in a state of anarchy, and happy will be the day when you British introduce law and order into Maharashtra and make Poona as safe as Bombay."

"Would you, then," I asked, "be willing to forego the sacred possession of liberty?"

"Liberty," he replied, "is not worth having when it means bloodshed and robbery and cruel oppression. Baji Rao is unworthy of the Brahmin caste which he disgraces and of the noble ancestors from whom he is descended. We may well say of him, in the words of our Maratha proverb, that he is one who, though born of a cow,[1] does the work of a butcher. Even in the Peshwa's capital we suffer the horrors of a sack whenever one faction wins the day over the other. The peasants have no care to cultivate their fields, knowing not who will gather the produce into barns. Such a government is bound to be overthrown by the gods, for well says the holy Tulasi Das:[2] 'Oppress not the poor, for the groans of the wretched bring retribution from heaven. The contemptible skin in time melts away the

[1] See Appendix, note 2. [2] See Appendix, note 3.

hardest iron.' Besides, we have not even the name of liberty, for the Peshwa is proud to call himself the Vakil-i-Mutlak[1] of the Great Mogul, who rules in Delhi. Why does not John Company[2] step in and be our emperor in the place of the Great Mogul? Then we should enjoy peace and prosperity, and every man would have at least the freedom of making his livelihood without fear of being plundered."

At this point our conversation was interrupted by a servant who came to light the lamp, and brought a message from my sepoy reminding me that the shades of night were falling fast, and that in the disturbed state of the city it would be excessively dangerous for us to pass through the streets after nightfall. So I took my leave, after Hari Rao had assured me that, if he could get any more information on the subject of my enquiry, he would communicate with me immediately.

[1] Vakil-i-Mutlak = chief minister.

[2] John Company is the name by which Indians spoke of the East India Company.

CHAPTER IX

DECOYED INTO THE PESHWA'S PALACE

WHEN we went out again into the street, and the gate was barred and chained behind us, the sun had already set, and the short Indian twilight was becoming rapidly dimmer. We began to ride rapidly in the direction of the cantonment, but had not proceeded far when I heard a voice say, in tones that seemed not unfamiliar to me:

"If the sahib would hear tidings of him that is lost, let him follow me."

The speaker was a native clothed in white flowing robes, whose face I could not see clearly in the dim light. As he spoke he moved away towards a narrow street on the right, leading in the direction of the centre of the native town. I naturally hesitated. Even without further delay there was considerable danger in our return to camp, and I had strict orders from my commanding officer to be back in good time. Then the stranger spoke again and said:

"If you fear to follow me, you may never have such a chance again."

Then there came over my mind the thought of Alice in the lonely tower of Rusko, mourning over her lost brother, and I hesitated no longer, but, accompanied by my faithful sepoy, plunged into the dark alley up which the mysterious stranger led us at a rapid pace. He hurried on so quickly that I could not conveniently question him, nor, however much I racked my brains, could I remember when and where I had heard his voice before, or guess how he had become acquainted with my purpose.

At last we stopped by a small door in a high wall. As the mysterious stranger stood in the recess enclosing the door, and began to open it, I jumped from my horse and, standing before him to prevent his escape, demanded to know who he was. Instead of replying, he hastily opened the door and ran in through it. I rushed in after him, leaving the two horses outside in charge of the sepoy.

I found myself in a garden, the atmosphere

B 592

"I FOUND MY DEPARTURE OBSTRUCTED BY THREE MEN"

of which was heavy with the perfume of the champak. The fugitive was too quick for me. He darted swiftly behind a clump of trees, and I stood alone in the garden, wondering to whom it belonged and why I had been decoyed there. Returning quickly to the door by which I had entered, I found my departure obstructed by three men, one of whom was coolly turning the key. I now saw clearly that I was entrapped, and called out to the sepoy over the wall to make off as fast as he could and save himself.

I then turned towards those who crossed my path, and asked them indignantly what right they had to stop me.

The tallest replied:

"Let me rather ask you what business you have in our lord the Peshwa's garden?"

"In the Peshwa's garden!" I exclaimed.

"Yes, sahib," he replied, "you are in the Peshwa's garden, and where you see that light burning the mighty prince is taking counsel with his advisers."

I was naturally surprised, not to say alarmed, at finding myself in such close proximity to the powerful and unscrupulous potentate on whose conduct it depended whether there should be peace or war in Western India.

"Why," I asked, "have I been decoyed here?"

"Because His Highness the Peshwa wishes to see you. I must now request you to follow me to his presence."

Resistance would have been futile. Even if I could have broken my way through the three men before me, the door was locked, and there were doubtless many more of the Peshwa's retainers within call. So I submitted to the force of circumstances, and was led into the palace.

CHAPTER X

BEFORE THE PESHWA

THE room in which the Peshwa was sitting was illuminated by two great chandeliers, the light of which was reflected from prismatic pendants and from innumerable small mirrors in the wood-work of the walls and ceiling. The Peshwa was seated in a corner of the room on a cushion of white muslin embroidered in coloured silk and ornamented with gold fringe. He himself was dressed in a robe of white muslin. A diamond aigrette of great price blazed in the front of his turban, and a triple necklace of pearls, with pendants of rubies and emeralds, hung round his neck. He was a remarkably handsome man. As he had no shoes or slippers on, I noticed the small size of his feet, of which he appeared to be very vain. His features were so regular and delicate that they seemed almost effeminate. In front of him, in attitudes of extreme deference, stood three of his principal nobles whom I afterwards was able to identify. They were Moro Dikshit, Bapu Gokhle, who was his commander-in-chief, and the notorious Trimbakji Danglia, who had murdered the Brahmin envoy from Baroda, in spite of the safe-conduct he had from the British Government. Like them, I stood before the Peshwa and waited to hear what he had to say. It was not long before my curiosity was satisfied.

"You are no doubt surprised," said the Peshwa, "to find yourself in our palace. Whether you remain in our hands as a prisoner or are treated as an honoured guest, will depend upon yourself alone."

He spoke with a smile that was intended to disarm suspicion. When he chose to win over a useful instrument to carry out his purposes, he could be as affable as it is possible for a proud prince to be. But I knew well, from what I had heard, that he was one of those who could smile and smile and smile and be a villain. Was he not the instigator of the audacious murder of Gangadhar Shastri in the holy city of Pandharpur? Was he not also the friend and the protector of the murderer? Had not those eyes, which now looked with apparent frankness and friendliness into mine, exulted joyfully at the sight of Vithoji Holkar trampled under the feet of elephants by his order in the streets of Poona? Remembering all this, I was on my guard and received with distrust the proposal that he now proceeded to make to me, all the more that it was introduced by a compliment couched in the vein of Oriental hyperbole.

"The fame of your learning," he went on, "came before you to Poona. We know that on the voyage out to Bombay you mastered the language of Maharashtra, which, marvellous to relate, you could speak like a native of the country before you had even placed your foot on the soil of India. We also know that you are familiarly acquainted with all the dead and living languages of Europe."

From this I could conjecture who it was that had decoyed me into the garden of the Vishram Bagh. It could be no other than Captain Dixon's Indian servant, who had taught me the Maratha language on board ship.

"Your Highness," I replied, "has been misinformed. I can lay no claim to the name of a scholar, although I have a smattering of a few foreign languages. However, such knowledge as I possess is at Your Majesty's service, so far as it may be without prejudice to the interests of His Britannic Majesty, of whom I am a humble but loyal servant."

I seemed to discern the shadow of a frown on the smooth surface of the Peshwa's brow, when he heard the qualification with which I concluded the offer of my services. However, he took no notice of it and proceeded.

"We also, in the intervals of respite from the heavy burdens of sovereignty, take some interest in learned men and their writings and discussions. Now one of our pundits has happened to find, by a strange chance, a manuscript written in an unknown script, which neither he nor any of his fellows can read. We should be glad if your learning may enable you to satisfy our curiosity by reading and interpreting it to us. If you can do so, you will no longer be our prisoner, but we will dismiss you with honour and gifts from our presence."

It was easy to see that the Peshwa was deceiving me. It was not likely that all this trouble had been taken to entrap me merely that I should satisfy the curiosity of the

Peshwa and his learned men as to the contents of a literary document. However, I requested to be allowed to see the manuscript, which was accordingly placed in my hands by Trimbakji Danglia.

It was all written in the Greek character. Otherwise it was a curious medley. Some of the sentences were written in good Greek prose, others consisted of English words written in Greek letters, while in other parts of the manuscript English and Greek words were mixed up together. It appeared to be a diary of political events of a very recent date. I knew that Mr. Mountstuart Elphinstone was, in his spare hours, a diligent student of the classical languages of Greece and Rome, and inferred that the diary was his. He had evidently employed the Greek alphabet as a convenient cipher, using English words when he happened to be in a hurry, and translating his notes into Greek prose when he had more time at his disposal. The most cursory inspection of the diary showed that it was a dangerous document for the Peshwa to have in his hands. It contained, among other matters, the record of the result of interviews with Maratha nobles, who would have reason to dread the vengeance of their master, if he were informed of the promises they had made, or even of the fact that they had had secret interviews with the British resident. It was therefore impossible for me to accede to the Peshwa's request.

For a moment I hesitated whether I should attempt to defeat cunning by cunning. Could I not give an imaginary translation that would endanger no one's head and would not reveal the plans of the British resident, who, as I was convinced, was the author of the diary? But I quickly dismissed the thought. In the first place, in the house of my father and mother the law of truth-speaking had been strictly observed, and all forms of lying were abhorrent to me. In the second place, I knew that I should prove a sorry dissembler, and that those with whom I had to deal, masters as they were in all the arts of dissimulation, would easily see through my feeble efforts to cast dust in their eyes. So I preferred the straightforward course, and after reading a page or two of the diary, informed the Peshwa that, if I were permitted to take the manuscript away with me, I would gladly send him, on the morrow, a translation of the whole of it, if my commanding officer made no objection to my doing so.

On hearing my answer, the Peshwa no longer deigned to conceal his haughty displeasure.

"You appear to forget," he said, "that you are our prisoner, and completely in our power. If you defy us—well, you will not be the only English officer immured in our dungeons."

I did not know whether he had in his mind British officers already languishing in Maratha dungeons, or whether he was counting upon those whom he would capture when he overwhelmed the small British force in Poona. I ventured to ask whether John Hannay was imprisoned in any part of his dominions. This remark of mine was a spark which made his smouldering rage burst into flame.

"That name," he cried in a sudden burst of fury that revealed the tiger in his nature, "is never mentioned in my presence by those who care much to live. Trimbakji," he added, turning to the most wicked and unscrupulous of his advisers, "take from our presence this young man who sets such small store on his life and liberty, and see whether your gentle methods cannot induce him to grant our request."

When he said this, one of his counsellors threw himself on his knees at the Peshwa's feet, and raised his closed hands in an attitude of supplication. But I did not hear what he said, for, before he finished the compliments with which an Oriental minister addresses his sovereign, I was taken out of the room.

CHAPTER XI

I ESCAPE OUT OF THE CLUTCHES OF TRIMBAKJI

TRIMBAKJI, supported by two of his myrmidons, who were waiting outside the door, now led me from the brightly illuminated presence chamber of the Peshwa to an underground apartment dimly lighted by a single oil-lamp. Here I was deprived of my sword, and my hands were tied behind my back with such unnecessary violence that the cords cut into my wrists.

It was terribly galling to find myself at the mercy of those unscrupulous villains. I tried to awe them by threatening them with British vengeance if they did not immediately desist from their violence and let me go.

"Remember," I said, "that we are not now at war, and that my detention as a prisoner is a breach of the law of nations. Although I am but a junior officer in the British army, yet if you touch a hair of my head, you need not hope to escape the punishment that will be your due. The arm of British justice is far-reaching, and will not allow the meanest subject of our king to suffer wrong with impunity."

"British vengeance has few terrors for me," replied Trimbakji with an evil sneer. "Perhaps you do not know that I am Trimbakji Danglia, who, under the protection of my lord the Peshwa, have defied the vengeance of the British so long, and broke through the walls of their strongest prison. You see me here at large, the deadly enemy of you and all your race, and, in spite of all your policy, the greatest name in the Dekhan, next to the mighty Peshwa, whose will you have dared to cross. But why bandy more words? Let us proceed to deeds. Bring forward," he called to his attendants, "the instruments of torture, and see if we cannot bend this young springald to the Peshwa's will."

In obedience to his order his two creatures brought forward some hideous instruments of wood and iron, the exact nature of which I could not determine in the half-lighted subterranean chamber to which I had been brought.

"Here," he said, "are persuasive counsellors, who will help you to come to a right decision in the choice that I am about to lay before you. Take service under the Peshwa, and rise to wealth and honour and high command in his army; or refuse, and condemn your corpse to be thrown to the dogs after suffering the most horrible tortures. Think not that either feelings of mercy or fear of British power will stay my hand. I am no such weakling. Have I not cut off the hands and feet of many of my own countrymen who provoked my anger, and shall I shrink from inflicting the same or worse mutilation on an obstinate foreigner, who is completely in my power, if he ventures to defy me and my master? Now, choose!"

There was but one answer to make. I made it, and waited for the torture to be applied, fortifying myself for the ordeal by the Epicurean consolation that great pains can last but a short time.

But Providence spared me from undergoing the torture which Trimbakji's devilry designed for me. His attendants had scarcely laid hands on me to take me to the rack, when the door of the chamber was opened, and there came into the room the tallest of the three Marathas who had obstructed my retreat in the garden. He immediately addressed Trimbakji, and said:

"His Highness the Peshwa has changed his mind with regard to the prisoner, and wishes to see him once more."

"This is your father's doing," angrily exclaimed Trimbakji. "Cursed be the day when the Peshwa gave such a weakling a place in his council and the command of his armies!"

By these words it was revealed to me that my deliverer was Govindrao Gokhle, the Maratha commander-in-chief's son, who had already won distinction among the younger warriors of the Dekhan. He made no answer to Trimbakji's rude taunt, but proceeded with tender care, that showed his sympathy, to unloose the bonds with which I had been bound hand and foot. He then led me out of the room, bidding me lean on his shoulder if I felt at all faint. Such kindness from a stranger touched my heart, and the more by contrast with the brutal treatment to which I had been subjected just before, and, shaken as I was by what I had undergone, I was glad of the support offered me by the friend whom I had found in the centre of a hostile court.

When I re-entered the presence-chamber

the anger of the Peshwa appeared to have vanished, and he received me with an ingratiating smile.

"We had heard much," he said, "of the steadfast loyalty of British soldiers, and wished to put it to as severe a test as possible. Nobly you have stood the test, and now are as gold tried by the fire. You are as faithful to your king and master as Sakharam Bapu was to our sire.[1] Such virtue we honour even in an enemy. You are from this moment free, and Govindrao Gokhle, the captain of our guard, shall conduct you in safety to your cantonments."

After thanking the Peshwa with gratitude, although perhaps not with as much humility as would satisfy the soul of an Oriental despot, I left the presence-chamber accompanied by young Gokhle. At the door we met Trimbakji, who gave us both a scowl of hatred. Then without delay Gokhle called his attendants to bring two horses. They were both of them fine strong specimens of the famous Bhimthari breed. He mounted me on the larger and handsomer of the two, and side by side we rode through the dark and deserted

[1] See Appendix, note 4.

streets in the direction of the British cantonment at Garpir.

In spite of difference of race and creed, in spite of the fact that we were soldiers belonging to armies that would probably in a short time meet each other in a deadly struggle, we seemed drawn together by a strong mutual attraction, and by tacit consent rode slowly, so that we might enjoy, while fate allowed us, the pleasure of companionship. Destiny had brought us together for the time being. In a short hour or less we should probably drift in different directions on the waves of fortune, and might never meet again. So we rode slowly through the streets of Poona, grudging the shortness of the time during which we were allowed to reap the fruits of our new friendship.

CHAPTER XII

AFFRAY IN THE STREETS OF POONA

WE were naturally disposed to form a mutual admiration society of two. I was impressed by the easy grace with which he managed his high-mettled, or I might even say somewhat vicious, horse. He could not get over my withstanding the Peshwa to his face, and my having mastered the Maratha language before landing in India.

"I had a good teacher," I explained, "in that rascal who decoyed me into the Peshwa's garden. How did he happen to turn up in Poona?"

"He is a Poona man. He was a servant of Captain Moore's, and I saw him often when that officer was a frequent guest at the Peshwa's court."

"Did you ever meet John Hannay?" I next asked.

"Only once," he replied, "just before his mysterious disappearance, of which I know no more than you do."

I besought him to give me any information that might help me to get to the bottom of the mystery, but he could only suggest that possibly the wily Maratha who had decoyed me into danger might throw some light upon the subject if it were made worth his while to do so.

I then asked him how it was that the Peshwa had changed his mind and let me go free. For I knew well, from the anger expressed by his words and countenance, that he had not delivered me over to the cruel hands of Trimbakji merely with the intention of testing by experiment whether the loyalty of British officers was or was not over-estimated.

"Directly you left the presence," replied young Gokhle, "my father threw himself at the Peshwa's feet and besought him to do you no harm, representing that there was no open war as yet between the British and the Marathas, and that His Highness's glory and the reputation of the Maratha nation would be tarnished by such a violation of humanity and the customs observed in the relations between civilized nations in war and in peace. He also pointed out that such an act would lead to bloody reprisals when war broke out, and that His Highness the Peshwa himself would be held personally responsible for any injury done to a British officer captured in time of peace and punished by his orders."

"Perhaps," I suggested, "the last consideration was of most avail, for I have heard that the present Peshwa is not endowed with the high courage that distinguished his warlike ancestors."

At this remark, which courtesy should perhaps have prevented me from making, Gokhle seemed annoyed. He did not, however, deny its truth, but contented himself with saying:

"His Highness the Peshwa has no occasion to fear reprisals. When he raises his golden standard and marshals in battle array the fifty thousand Marathas who are here to defend his throne, he will overwhelm in a moment your small force, and drive your sepoys and your Englishmen from the Dekhan and the Konkan back to Bombay as easily as the strong monsoon wind drives away a swarm of locusts."

"No one disputes," I replied, "the value of the Maratha horsemen, but they were six to one against us at Assaye, and their numbers and valour did not save them from defeat."

This discussion, which, if prolonged, might have endangered our new-formed friendship, was at this point rudely interrupted. Our too leisurely ride was suddenly obstructed by four well-mounted horsemen. Their leader, whose face was concealed by a mask, called upon us in a loud voice to stand in the name of the Peshwa.

"Show me first," replied Gokhle, "some token that you have really the authority of His Highness. In these days of confusion many claim to speak in the Peshwa's name who have no better authority to do so than I have."

"Here," replied the masked man, "is the Peshwa's order, dated this day, authorizing me to arrest any British officer found in the streets of Poona after dark."

Gokhle inspected the document coolly, and replied:

"This seems a genuine order, but I have come straight from the presence of His Highness with orders to accompany this officer to the British cantonments."

"If you resist my order," the unknown replied, "your blood be on your own head."

He then ordered his three followers to lay hands upon me. I immediately drew my sword to defend myself, and Gokhle did likewise.

By a lucky cut I succeeded in disabling the

sword-arm of the foremost of our enemies, who had seized my bridle-rein. The wounded man seemed only too glad to retire from the combat. Thus the disparity in our numbers was reduced so considerably that their masked leader, who at first seemed disposed to hold aloof, was constrained to take part in the fray. Gokhle called to me to ride off at full speed to the cantonment, and he would keep our three remaining assailants at bay. Of course I refused to disgrace myself by leaving him alone in such a dangerous position. So we fought on, two against three, by the misty light of the rising moon.

The fight was not so unequal as might have been expected, for our enemies did not appear to be willing to risk their lives, and even their leader showed more energy in shouting words of encouragement and curses to his followers than in delivering blows with his own hand. By superior strength I pulled one man off his horse and hurled him to the ground, where he lay stunned in the gutter beside the road. At the same moment Gokhle got close up to the man in the mask, and, pulling the disguise from his face, revealed to view the ill-omened visage of Trimbakji Danglia.

This put an end to the scuffle. When Trimbakji was stripped of his disguise, he did not venture to carry out his audacious design of seizing one who was by the Peshwa's express orders being escorted through the streets of Poona by the son of the Peshwa's commander-in-chief. Without a word, but not without a look of deadly anger, he called off his men and allowed us to proceed on our way in peace.

For the rest of our way we were unmolested. The streets through which we passed were as absolutely deserted as if Poona had been a city of the dead. The state of the city was not such as to encourage marriage processions or other forms of peaceful festivity. The shops were closed with firmly barred doors and shutters, and all who had anything to lose trembled for the safety of their possessions and remained in their houses. The Maratha soldiery were in their quarters, where they indulged in wild revelry and celebrated the triumph they anticipated when they should at last be led against the enemy.

When we reached the British cantonment at Garpir, I asked Govindrao Gokhle whether he would take away with him the horse I had ridden, or whether I should send it back on the morrow.

"No," he replied. "You must accept black Moti as a pledge of our friendship if you will accept me as a friend. If in the war that is imminent your side should win, then you must afford to me such kindness as the victor may show to the vanquished, and I on my part swear to do the same if the arms of the Peshwa triumph, as they surely will."

Looking at the matter from the light of subsequent events, one might suppose that Govindrao Gokhle was offering me his good horse as a bribe to secure his safety in the hour of defeat. But this would be an entirely wrong view. Govindrao Gokhle never for a moment feared that the large army commanded by his father would not easily overpower the two thousand British troops in Poona. It was only out of courtesy that he spoke to me as if there were a possibility of the British winning a victory. His proposal was, in fact, merely a delicate way of offering me protection in the hour of Maratha triumph, which he regarded as absolutely certain. He had already, in our conversation, revealed his firm conviction of the overwhelming superiority of the Maratha forces, and he showed the same confidence again by his answer to me when I expressed my reluctance to deprive him of the fine horse that he offered me. I asked him whether he thought it consistent with his duty to the Peshwa that he should present such a noble steed to an officer in the British army.

"One man, however valiant, and one horse, were it Rana Pertab's Chetak," he replied, "will make little difference in the coming battle, when fifty thousand cavaliers of Maharashtra assail your encampment. Let others seek to filch a victory by underhand means. My noble father is confident in the justice of our cause, and in the number and courage of the warriors who will follow him to battle. Therefore he besought his master, the Peshwa, to let you go free, and therefore his son begs you to accept this horse, no unworthy gift for a brave enemy, for in good truth it would be difficult to find a fleeter horse than Moti through the length and breadth of the Dekhan."

So I accepted it, and bade my chivalrous friend and enemy a hearty farewell.

CHAPTER XIII

MY INTERVIEW WITH MR. ELPHINSTONE

AS soon as I entered the cantonment I repaired to Colonel Burr's quarters and gave him a short account of my adventures. He considered the information I had brought to be of such importance that he ordered me immediately to go and report all I had seen and heard to Mr. Mountstuart Elphinstone, the British resident at Poona, who lived in the Residency at the Sangam or junction of the rivers Mutha and Mula, about a mile from the Garpir cantonment.

When I arrived at the Residency I was immediately taken to the presence of Mr. Mountstuart Elphinstone. I found him on the veranda of his bungalow, bending over the balustrade and looking in the direction of the native city, as if to divine from its silence, or from such sounds as reached his ear, what the Marathas were doing or contemplating. It was with much interest that now, for the first time, I looked upon the famous Indian civilian of whom I had heard so much, and his personal appearance did not disappoint my expectations. A physiognomist might have conjectured from his face that he was a man of high birth, of a subtle intellect, and dauntless courage. He had a high forehead, and his refined features, which, chiselled by Chantrey and painted by Lawrence, still give delight in Bombay to lovers of the fine arts, were such as might naturally be supposed to give evidence of a long line of distinguished ancestors.

He advanced to meet me, and, shaking me kindly by the hand, gave me a warm greeting before asking me a question about the news I had brought.

"Some weeks ago," he said, "a letter came to me from my old friend Mr. MacCulloch, telling me that he had a nephew coming to India, and asking me to show him any kindness in my power. As the nephew of Mr. MacCulloch you are heartily welcome. That is quite enough recommendation. But he tells me you are a scholar, and on that account you are doubly welcome, for I too delight in the classics; and, when these troubles are over, you and Dr. Jeffreys and Captain Close and I will enjoy many a delightful conversation on the great authors of Greece and Rome. But you will take some refreshment before you tell me what has brought you here at this late hour."

For Mr. Elphinstone, although himself mos abstemious in eating and drinking, respected the weaknesses of his fellow-men, and was not wanting in the hospitality for which a past generation of Anglo-Indians was deservedly famous.

I replied that, with his permission, I would relate my experiences in the city of Poona first, and that afterwards I should be most glad of a little refreshment. So Mr. Elphinstone ordered me some supper, and, while it was being prepared, he listened attentively to what I had to say, here and there asking me pertinent questions which showed his intimate familiarity with Maratha manners and customs and with the intrigues of the Peshwa's court.

As I had conjectured, the Greek document that had fallen into the hands of the Peshwa and his ministers was Mr. Elphinstone's private diary. When I expressed regret that I had not been able to throw dust in the Peshwa's eyes by giving a false translation or account of the diary, he commended me, saying:

"You are too young to smirch your soul with a falsehood; nor would it have availed you much. Oppose the cunning of these wily Marathas with cunning and you will be outmatched and ignominiously defeated. But again and again in Indian history the cunning intrigues of Oriental Machiavellianism have been shattered by an Englishman's straightforward honesty, as the earthen pots in the fable were broken by the pots of brass. Cunning, as Bacon well says, is the ability of the weaker animal. It may win a few ephemeral victories, but in the long run must yield to truth and honesty. Therefore, my diplomatic motto has always been that contained in two lines of Homer, which no doubt you know well:

[1]*Ἐχθρὸς γάρ μοι κεῖνος ὁμῶς Ἀΐδαο πυλῃσιν,*
Ὅς χ᾽ ἕτερον μὲν κεύθῃ ἐνὶ φρεσὶν ἄλλο δὲ βάζει.

"Is there then no danger," I asked, "that someone may be found able to read your diary?"

"Not in Poona, I think, except my friend

1 "That man is hateful to me as the gates of Hell,
Who hides one thing in his heart and says another."

Dr. Jeffreys, and they will hardly be able to bribe him to be a traitor, however much they may try."

The most important information in my report was the intelligence of the presence of Trimbakji in Poona.

"I thought," he said, "that he was leading the insurgents on the frontier. If the Peshwa has ventured to summon that infamous outlaw to his presence, open war will not long be delayed. However, from what you tell me of the state of the city, and from the similar intelligence I have received from others, we need not fear a night attack. Go, then, and take some supper, and mind you retire early to bed, so that you may have a good rest after your adventures. Every Briton in Poona must nurse his strength for the struggle that is surely impending."

"May I first be allowed to enquire," I asked, "whom you suspect of having stolen your private diary?"

"Ah," he said, "that must be looked into! It must have been one of my domestic servants. No stranger could have entered my study without the certainty of being detected."

"May the thief not have been Captain

Dixon's servant, who showed his taste for plotting by inveigling me into the Peshwa's garden?"

"What was his name?"

"Haibati," I replied.

"I have no servant of that name in the Residency. But stay! what was the name of the new hamal I engaged the day before yesterday?"

The Mahometan butler being summoned, said that Narayan was the name of the new servant.

"Call him to my presence," said Mr. Elphinstone, and asked me, in the meantime, particulars about the height and general appearance of Haibati.

I could only describe him as being short and unusually fat for a native domestic servant.

"The new servant I engaged," Mr. Elphinstone said, "was also short and fat. He had a most laudatory character, written in an excellent handwriting, given him by a Bombay merchant, who died two months ago."

At this moment the butler returned with the information that the new servant was nowhere to be found, and had not been seen in the house since sunset.

"He is the man," said Mr. Elphinstone. "Could he write English?"

"Yes," I replied, "he wrote excellent English in a beautiful clerkly hand."

"No doubt he forged the character that purported to be written by the late Mr. Bateson, whose handwriting is unknown to me."

He then asked the butler whether the missing servant had left any possessions in the servants' quarters. The reply was that he had brought a very heavy box with him when he arrived, but that coolies had taken it away that very afternoon.

"All this gives a strong presumption of his guilt," remarked Mr. Elphinstone. "But that, after all, is a matter of no consequence. Unfortunately, the chief point is that the diary is gone, and cannot be recovered. But never mind! Long before it can be deciphered, I prophesy that the Peshwa will be a captive or a fugitive, whose vengeance no one need dread."

After this I took the excellent supper that Mr. Elphinstone's hospitality provided for me, and departed.

CHAPTER XIV

HAIBATI'S INFORMATION

TWO days after—that is on November 1—Mr. Elphinstone moved the British troops, now amounting to twelve hundred Sepoys and eight hundred Europeans, to Kirki, a suburb four miles to the north of Poona, leaving a company to defend the old cantonment at Garpir, and retaining a force of two hundred and fifty men to garrison the Residency at the Sangam. This made our position much more secure. The cantonment at Garpir was close to the city, and surrounded by gardens and great hedges of prickly-pear, behind which an enemy could find plenty of cover, and steal up unobserved to attack us. In the new position at Kirki we had a long stretch of open country between us and Poona, so that we were no longer exposed to the danger of being surprised by a sudden attack. The only disadvantage of the change of position was that it was attributed to fear, and raised the spirits of the Maratha warriors, so that they became even more confident of victory than they were before.

On the morning of November 2, as I was taking a walk in the neighbourhood of the camp, and enjoying the crisp freshness of the air of the Dekhan, I came upon a strange figure of a man seated cross-legged on a piece of matting by the roadside. His face was smeared with ashes, and the principal part of his apparel was an antelope-skin, which protected his body against the sharp morning air. His long hair was coiled into a great knot on the top of his head. As I approached him, he appeared to be telling devoutly the beads of the large rosary that hung round his neck. However, he raised his eyes, greeted me in the whining sing-song in which an Indian beggar solicits alms, and held out his begging-bowl, made of the shell of a cocoa-nut. I threw into it a small coin, and was proceeding to move on, when the ascetic, in the same whining voice, said to me:

"The sahib is an officer of the British army. This poor ascetic is a lover of the British, and has important news that nearly concerns the British Resident. But before I speak a word more, the sahib must swear to protect me against the danger I run by speaking; otherwise I am dumb."

On hearing these words I approached a few steps nearer him, half intending to make sure of his secret by seizing him. But he leapt on his feet suddenly, and said quickly, in tones very unlike the drawl in which he had previously addressed me:

"Advance a pace nearer, and I will fly away as swiftly as the antelope whose skin is wrapped round my shoulders. Even if you caught me, my whole body is anointed with oil, and would elude your grasp."

So I stood still, and asked him to tell me what he had to say, and assured him that the British Government was willing and able to protect its friends and well-wishers.

"Nay, but swear," he said. "Swear your most sacred oath, by God and the Son of God, by your hope of heaven and your fear of hell, that you will stand by me, if my life is threatened. Swear, too, that the British Government will reward me with rupees according to the value of the information that I give, and that, if the British Government fails to reward me, you yourself will pay me one thousand rupees."

"What," I asked, "does an ascetic want with money?"

"A thousand rupees will build me a shrine for the god whom I most adore. But that is my business. Will you swear as I bid you?"

"I swear that the British Government will protect you and reward you, if your information is really of importance."

"Swear it by the holy name of God," he said. I took the solemn oath he demanded, upon which he resumed his seat on the matting before me.

"Know then," he said, "that the Peshwa and Trimbakji Danglia have formed a plot to assassinate Elphinstone Sahib when he is taking his ride early to-morrow morning. I heard them arrange it all. When I was counting my beads in the garden of the Peshwa's palace, I saw them go to the summer-house for a secret conference. Stealthily as a snake I crept up to the window and overheard fragments of their conversation. If I had been detected, death would have been my lot, for the impious Trimbakji would not have regarded my holy life. Did he not once say that, if his master bade him, he would even kill a cow?"[1]

[1] See Appendix, note 2.

"Never mind," I said, "the danger to your own life, but tell me clearly how the life of Mr. Elphinstone, the British Resident, is to be assailed."

"Even the poor ascetic," he replied, "may attach value to his own frail life, although frequent fasting may have reduced him to a shadow of skin and bone."

I could not help smiling at this remark, for the rounded contours of a well-fed body were only half-concealed by the man's covering of antelope-skin. However, I forbore to offend him by pointing out the inconsistency, and asked him to give me further details of the conversation that he had overheard.

"The conversation took place," he said, "yesterday afternoon. Much of it I could not hear. It was, however, quite plain that they were laying a plot to assassinate the Resident. I heard distinctly, more than once, the words, 'The day after to-morrow', and 'Morning ride'. All know that Elphinstone Sahib rides out for exercise very early in the morning, and that he nearly always takes the road past Ganesh Khind. He is often alone and unattended, so that he invites attack."

"Did you catch no more words in the conversation? The slightest word that you remember may help us to defeat the hellish plot."

"The other words of importance that I heard were 'daggers' and 'Hirwa Bungalow', from which we may conjecture that the ambush will be laid in the neighbourhood of the Hirwa Bungalow, and that the assassins will be armed with daggers."

"Where is the Hirwa Bungalow?" I asked.

"It is a large unoccupied house about halfway between the temple of Ganesh Khind and the Sangam, and is called the Hirwa Bungalow because it is, or was once, painted green."

"Did you hear nothing else?"

"Only that Gokhle, the commander-in-chief, was not to be taken into the secret. It appeared that he had been sounded on the subject before, and expressed his abhorrence of assassination. 'He is one of those', said the Peshwa, 'who, though they desire an end, shrink from employing the most convenient means.'"

"You can tell me no more to throw light on the plot?"

"Nothing more, sahib."

"Then, before we part, give me your name,

that, when you claim your reward, I may know you."

"Nay, sahib," he replied, "someone else might take my name and claim the reward due to me. Better give me the gold stud in your collar, and see that the reward is given to whosoever brings that token."

I was somewhat surprised that he should know and guess that there was a gold stud concealed behind my neck-tie. As it was engraved with three boars' heads, the arms of our family, it was an excellent token that could not easily be mistaken or forged by an impostor, so I gave it to him.

As he took it in his hands, he remarked:

"The sahib seems to wonder that I should see what is concealed behind his neck-tie. But we ascetics, who devote ourselves to austerities and contemplation of the unseen world, have strange powers of insight conferred on us by the immortal gods. I am but a poor ascetic, but methinks I could tell the sahib more of his past and his future than is known to Elphinstone Sahib himself, though he is endowed with all the wisdom and learning taught in Feringhi schools."

"Tell me something of the past," I replied,

"and I will be willing to credit what you say of my future."

"You have come," he said, "from a distant land to search for a lost friend; but, as I look into your soul, I see that mixed with friendship is a deeper feeling urging you to persevere in your search."

In a moment flashed on my mind the knowledge of who he was.

"You villain!" I cried; "you are no ascetic, but the rogue who duped me and put me in the power of the Peshwa and his myrmidons!"

So speaking, I raised my cane as if I would strike him. He remained perfectly motionless, and calmly replied:

"The sahib gave his solemn promise to protect me, and must dismiss his anger against this poor man, who intended to do him good. For if the sahib had condescended to read the document written in strange characters, the Peshwa would have dismissed him with honour and rich rewards."

"How am I to trust you? You are a double-dyed traitor! You first betrayed me, and now you have betrayed your new patrons, the Peshwa and his ministers."

"You may trust me," he replied with an

angry look, "if you believe revenge to be strong among the passions that actuate men. I served the Peshwa and his ministers because they were my countrymen and promised me great rewards. I now serve the sahib log[1] because they will reward me, and because the Peshwa and Trimbakji have done me cruel wrong. For when I claimed the reward that I had fairly earned, they spurned me from their presence. Trimbakji Danglia scourged me with his riding-whip for daring to press my just claim."

Here he showed a cruel weal on his right leg.

"Trimbakji gave me this cut on the leg, and the Peshwa stood by and smiled when I howled with pain. Therefore will I rejoice when the Peshwa is hurled from his throne and Trimbakji is chained in the deepest and darkest dungeon in the Fort of Bombay. For well I know that this is their fate. Have I not been in the great city of London, and seen the power and multitude of the sahib log. I have more to tell you about your own quest, and will help you in that too, if you promise me a fair guerdon for my trouble. Your

[1] Sahib log = the ruling people, *i.e.* in India, the British.

friend John—— Go on thy way, sahib," he continued, suddenly changing his voice to the whining tone in which he had first addressed me, "after dropping some alms, however small, in the begging-bowl of the poor ascetic."

I saw two Maratha horsemen coming along the road, and took the hint. He was evidently afraid that our colloquy might attract the suspicion of the new-comers, so I dropped a piece of copper money into his begging-bowl and walked away back to the camp. An hour or two later I went out again in the hope of finding Haibati again in the same place, and hearing what he had to tell me about John Hannay, but he was gone.

CHAPTER XV

THE HIRWA BUNGALOW

THAT evening I was invited by Mr. Elphinstone to dine and sleep at the Residency. I thought it would be a good thing to take with me the tunic of chain-armour that my uncle had presented to me when I left Bombay. If he would consent to wear it under his shirt, it might prove a more efficient protection against assassination than his mounted body-guard. Before starting to ride over to the Residency I myself put on the chain-mail, either because that was the most convenient way to carry it, or because I had some presentiment of coming danger. I rode round by Ganesh Khind in order that on my way I might have a look at the house which had been selected as the most suitable place for the intended assassination.

Before I reached the Hirwa Bungalow the sun had set, and it was beginning to be dark. From an artistic point of view, at any rate, the deserted house and its surroundings were well contrived to be the scene of secret murder. As I rode slowly up to it, I could see over the broken weather-stained wall of the compound a great ugly house, part of the roof of which had fallen in. The garden in front was overgrown by the multitudinous trunks of a great banyan-tree, and the drive leading to the door was covered with rank vegetation. The half-broken shutters of the windows and the leaves of a solitary Palmyra palm-tree rattled in the fitful gusts of a strong north wind that happened to be blowing. As I passed the rotting gate of the compound, with my feelings wrought upon by all that was present to my senses and imagination, a light flashed from one of the windows of the house and a loud cry for help in a woman's voice suddenly broke through the startled air.

To jump from my saddle, fasten my horse to a tree, and burst in through the rickety gate was the work of a moment. I hurried along the path leading to the front of the house, but ere I reached the steps my ribs were bruised with blows delivered by masked men, who rushed at me from the gloom on either side. The weapons driven against me were daggers, which would have pierced my vital organs but for the strength of the coat of mail that I had put on.

I hastily drew my sword and dealt one of the villains on my right a blow on the head that stretched him on the ground. Then I rushed up the steps, and, taking my stand on the top, in front of the door of the house, rapidly took stock of my enemies. Three were left now. As they appeared to be armed only with long knives, I had a fair chance of defending myself against them, if only no other enemies came to the open door behind me and attacked me in the rear. One of the ruffians cried out:

"This is not Elphinstone Sahib; look at his moustache, his soldier's clothes. Why should we kill him? We have made a mistake; let us go."

"No," said the one who seemed to be their leader. "What does it matter? If he is a British officer, the Peshwa will reward us for killing him."

So they all came up the steps to attack me. By rapid movements of my sword I kept them at bay for some time. At last, when a good opportunity presented itself, I dashed forward

D 392

"I KEPT THEM AT BAY FOR SOME TIME"

and struck the nearest of my assailants a blow, placed him *hors de combat*, and reduced my enemies to two. But, alas! such was the violence of the concussion with his thick skull that my sword broke off at the hilt, and to save my life no resource was left but instant flight. I had to submit to the indignity of turning my back on the ruffians, and ran along the passage into the middle of the house in the hope of finding some exit at the other side. My two remaining foes rushed after me, and I appeared to have little chance of escape. The passage led into a quadrangle, shut in on every side. I was caught like a rat in a trap.

Just, however, as I was, in my despair, about to turn and do my best to contend with my naked fists against the daggers of the assassins, a female voice from behind a half-closed door called out to me: "Come in here—it is your only chance!" I accepted the invitation, and, pushing through the door, found the room occupied by a woman, who immediately, with my help, ran the bolt of the door into the staple, and thus, for the moment, I was safe.

As soon as I had recovered my breath I

turned round to see who it was that had thus, like a god in a Greek tragedy, intervened to save me when death appeared inevitable.

"Who are you, fair lady?" I asked; "and what has moved you to come to my aid when death stared me in the face? Was it your voice that called for help, and did these villains attack you before my arrival turned their attention to me?"

"First," she replied, "the sahib must look to the defences of the room. Your honour can hardly listen calmly to my tale when ruffians are waiting outside, thirsting for your blood, and you have nothing to defend yourself with but the hilt of a broken sword."

"I am not so defenceless as you think," I said, drawing my pistol from the pocket in which it was concealed, and loading it. "Now that I have had time to charge this little weapon, I can well hold my own against those who seek my life. The door is barred, and anyone who shows his head through either of the two windows may be pretty sure of getting a bullet in his brain. So, now that that is satisfactorily arranged, I should be much obliged if you, fair lady, would explain how matters stand, and I will be careful to keep my eye upon the two windows. But first let me see the face of the lady to whom I owe my life."

"It is not for me, shameless as I am," she said, "to act the part of a shamefaced maiden."

So speaking, she suddenly tore her veil from her face and revealed to view, by the red light of the after-glow which illumined the room from the window on the west, the most beautiful face I ever saw in India. Her complexion was of the purest olive, and, in spite of what she said, it was suffused by a deep blush, betokening the feeling of shame that she professed to have lost. Her face had lost the rounded contours of youth and good health, although she was still very young; but what might have seemed a defect in another only brought out in clearer lines her delicate features and the perfectly modelled shape of her head. It was like the face of a woman who had in a few years lived a life of passion and excitement, of one who had perhaps sinned and suffered much. Add to all this that her eyes were deep brown; that, to set off their brightness, her eyelashes were slightly coloured with black unguent; and that her hair was black as night, and you may perhaps form an idea of the vision that burst upon my eyes when she drew her veil aside. For the information of any ladies who may deign to read my story, I should mention that she was clothed in a heavy garment of embroidered silk, and had ear-rings of diamonds, and on her nose a jewel composed of several large pearls.

"It was my voice that cried for aid," she said. "I knew my cry was to help in carrying out a murderous plot; they told me that, by coming here and doing what they bade me, I should in some strange way help to secure the freedom of my country. I did not refuse, for I had much to atone for, and thought the gods would pardon my wickedness if I helped the cause of my country's freedom. It was first arranged that I should come here to-morrow morning, and then, for some reason unknown to me, the plan was changed, and I came here this afternoon. As directed, I shouted, as loud as I could, a cry of agony, and you know what happened afterwards. It seems they intended to kill Elphinstone Sahib, who ventures to dictate laws to the mighty Peshwa; but you came first, and were, I suppose, in the dimness of the twilight and the excitement of the moment mistaken for him. I know no more."

"Then how was it," I asked, "that your heart moved you to save him whom your voice had lured to destruction?"

"Is my heart made of stone?" she replied. "Am I not a woman? Could I look on without pity and see even you, one of the enemies of my country, cruelly done to death before my eyes. But look—the window!" she exclaimed.

A head appeared, but, before I could fire, it dropped out of sight; voices were heard below the window. "Listen," said the lady. "Alas, others have joined them! Methinks I hear the voice of Trimbakji himself."

However, no other head ventured to show itself above the window-sill. The attack was made, after a few minutes' pause, upon the door, and a dangerous attack it was, with a great beam used as a battering-ram, which made the strong panels creak and all the bolts rattle ominously. It was not long before the point of the beam came crashing through the timbers and protruded into the room.

"The first man who enters dies!" I cried; but my threats had little effect, and the door would soon have been smashed to pieces. Suddenly, however, the crashing noise ceased. Something had evidently disturbed the operations of our assailants. It was not long before the cause of the interruption was made known to us. A voice from outside, that I easily recognized to be Mr. Elphinstone's, was heard calling out:

"Is anyone inside?"

I quickly drew the bolt, and saw before me Mr. Elphinstone, a military officer, and three native cavalry sepoys. Mutual explanations were hastily given and received. I told my story in as few words as I could, while we walked to the gate. The lady was mounted on the horse of one of the native troopers, who walked by her side. While riding slowly towards the Sangam, Mr. Elphinstone told me that in the afternoon he had ridden over to Major Ford, who commanded the Peshwa's subsidiary battalion at Dapuri, six miles from Poona. Major Ford had come back with him to dine at the Residency, and had fortunately insisted on bringing two mounted sepoys with him.

As they passed the Hirwa Bungalow they heard loud shouts and the crashing of the beam against the door. So they dismounted, and rushed in to see what was the matter. The assassins, on seeing them come, hastily dropped the beam that they were using as a battering-ram and fled into the dark shade of the trees round the bungalow.

CHAPTER XVI

HIRA'S STORY

WHEN we arrived at the Sangam, Mr. Elphinstone at once gave orders that a palanquin should be prepared for the lady that had played such an important part in that afternoon's adventure. When she was asked whither she would wish to be conducted, she replied that she would like first to disburden her mind of secret knowledge that nearly concerned me, and prayed that she might have a private interview with me for a few minutes.

Major Ford whispered a word of warning to me:—

"Take care that she has not a poisoned dagger concealed in her sleeve. You had better not trust yourself alone with her."

Through her veil, with a woman's quick intuition, she half-heard the whisper, and said:

"Weak women, such as I am, may slay

strong warriors when, as the poet says, a leaf of the blue lotos can cleave the hard wood Sami. You need not fear for your friend. Daggers of steel are not the weapons that I have used aforetime to effect my purposes, nor will I resort to them now. And why should I try to take away the life that I saved but an hour ago? If, however, you fear a weak woman, let me tell my tale to him at the end of this veranda, and let the young man take his loaded pistol and shoot me dead if I make a suspicious movement."

In accordance with her proposal I went with her to the end of the veranda, but I scorned to think of defending myself against a woman to whom I owed my life.

"I thank you, sir, for trusting me," she said with a sweet smile; "and, as you do not treat me like a tigress, I can better tell you what I have to say. Though I shall relate much that will cover me with shame, I must unveil myself that you may clearly hear and understand all my story."

On this she once more drew aside her veil, and I saw that, since we left the Hirwa Bungalow, she had been weeping bitterly.

"First," she said, "I must ask you whether

I am right in supposing that it was you that were in the Budhwar Palace last Thursday, and in the Peshwa's presence mentioned the name of John Hannay?"

I answered in the affirmative.

"You asked for information about his disappearance?"

"I did so," I replied, "for it was chiefly to search for him that I came to this far-away land."

"And why," she asked, "are you so eager to find him?"

"Firstly, because he was my dearest friend; and secondly, for I will conceal nothing from the lady whose pity saved me from the daggers of assassins, because he was the brother of her whom I love most in the world, and whom some day I hope to make my bride."

"Do you think that your friend is dead?"

"I do not know," I replied, "whether he is dead or alive. Only, from what I heard in the Budhwar Palace, it appears that somehow he terribly offended the Peshwa, and that little is all I have learnt to clear up the mystery of his disappearance."

"Then this much, if you will deign to

hear my story, I may add to your knowledge. I can tell you how your friend incurred the Peshwa's deadly hatred. He lives somewhere in one of His Highness's prisons. Where his place of confinement is I cannot tell. But why should I say more? My tale is a painful one to tell, and will not, I fear, enable you to find him who is lost."

"Nay, lady," I replied, "endure to tell it. All that has happened to John Hannay cannot but be of the deepest interest to his friend and to his father and sister, who are now mourning for him as one mourns for the dead."

"Hear, then," she said, "the story of the unhappy Hira. But that is not my real name. Let my true name be forgotten, so that I may not bring disgrace to the noble family to which I belonged. But in the Peshwa's court my flatterers called me Hira, because, they said, I shone like a precious stone in the Peshwa's diadem. Seeing me now, after a year of sin and sorrow, you would hardly believe that my beauty was once conspicuous in a mighty prince's court. But so it was."

"Nay," I replied, "I can well believe it,

for when you took off your veil in the Hirwa Bungalow your face was like the morning star emerging from behind a cloud."

"Ah, well!" she said, "if I had beauty, it was my curse, and brought ruin also on your friend, the fair-haired boy, who stood forth so bravely as my champion, and all in vain. Had it not been for my fatal gift of beauty, I should never have attracted the eye of the Peshwa. I should have married the brave young warrior to whom I was betrothed, and not disgraced my family and my name. How well I remember the day that was the beginning of my evil fortune! I was then happy and innocent, and, though a girl,[1] the pride of my father's house. My parents had betrothed me to a Maratha noble, who had a high office in the Peshwa's court.

"You must have passed through the village of Chinchwad on your way from Bombay to Poona. There my father, and the sirdar to whom I was betrothed, and many of my relations lived. One evening, after the rains, just one year ago, I was returning home from a visit to a relation who lived in the country a few miles from the town. The

[1] See Appendix, note 5.

Peshwa and some of his courtiers were expected in Chinchwad that evening to attend the annual fair in honour of Ganpati, and the bearers of my palanquin were directed to keep out of their course, for his licentiousness was well known and dreaded by his subjects. They therefore took me most of the way by a side-path, but it was necessary to join the main road at a distance of about a mile from the town. It was a beautiful evening, and the setting sun was encircled with great golden clouds of fantastic form. I told the bearers to set the palanquin down, and drew the curtains, in order that I might for a few minutes enjoy the beauty of the scene. How well I remember it all! It was the sunset of my happy girlhood. My heart was full of joy and thankfulness, and since then, although I have engaged wildly in the vain pursuit of pleasure, I have never enjoyed an hour of peace of mind and real happiness.

"As I was drinking in the beauty of the scene, a richly-attired cavalier appeared in sight, coming from the direction of Poona. I hastily drew the curtains of my palanquin, and bade the bearers raise me from the ground and carry me home. But before they could do so, the cavalier rode up, and in a commanding voice ordered them to stand still. Then he pulled aside the curtain of the palanquin, and said to me:

"'Allow me, fair lady, to look more closely on the beauty of thy countenance, which, as I approached, the envious curtain screened from my view, even as yonder golden clouds shroud the brilliance of the setting sun.'

"I was overwhelmed with shame, and knew not what to say or do, except to cover my face with my hands. Even so, he would not desist, but, dismounting, gave his horse to one of my bearers to hold. He then laid his hand on mine, and tried to compel me by force to uncover my face. His rudeness and violence made me burst into tears. I passionately called upon my bearers to defend me, but they feared to face the anger of one who appeared by his rich dress and arms to be a great noble.

"I do not know what would have happened, had not another cavalier appeared on the scene. He was as splendidly attired as my persecutor, although in a different style, which moved my wonder, for I had never seen a man so dressed before. He was clad in a tight-fitting tunic of dark-blue with yellow facings and slashed with silver. His face still more excited my wonder on account of its whiteness and the redness of his cheeks. I had never seen such a man before, but I conjectured rightly that he was an officer of one of the British regiments then stationed in Poona."

"You have described exactly," I said, "the uniform of the 18th Hussars, to which John Hannay belonged. The new-comer can have been none other than John Hannay, unless it was Captain Moore, who is an officer in the same regiment."

"It was," she said, "as I afterwards learnt, the unfortunate John Hannay. You know how fair and handsome he was, and you may well imagine that to me who had never before seen a Feringhi he looked like a being come from another world to protect me from wrong. I held out my hands to him in supplication, and he lent an ear to my prayer, for he rode up to my persecutor and spoke angry words to him. The Maratha noble scarcely seemed to believe his ears when he heard himself addressed in this fashion. With a contemptuous curl of his upper lip he took me by the hand as if he would lead me out of the palanquin. Then my defender smote him with his whip across the face, and, drawing his sword, placed himself in a posture of defence, as if he were waiting for the other to mount his horse and engage him in single combat. The rage of the proud Maratha, on feeling the lash of the officer's whip on his cheek, was something terrible to contemplate. Using terms of fearful abuse, he mounted his horse and rode with drawn sword at the British officer, as if he would sweep him off the face of the earth. But when his enemy stood calm and motionless as a marble statue, his heart failed him, and he pulled up his horse so as to avoid the combat. Then he cried out:

"'Dog of a Feringhi, the PESHWA will not pollute his sword with your low-born blood, but be sure that his vengeance will lie in wait for you and dog your footsteps, and that you will soon curse the day when you dared to cross the path of the mightiest prince or India."

"With that he rode away, looking back once or twice, as if he feared that he might be pursued. Presently I saw him at some distance rejoin his train of courtiers and escort, whom he had temporarily left for some caprice of his own. In the meantime my bearers had lifted me in my palanquin and borne me to my home. My preserver escorted me part of the way, and tried to comfort me and calm my terrors by speaking kindly words to me in his own language.

"You have now heard how your friend incurred the wrath of the mighty Peshwa by nobly succouring the oppressed. It shames me to tell the miserable sequel of the story, as far as I myself am concerned. Fain, fain would I be silent and tell no more. The Peshwa was foiled for the time being, but gained his object in the end. Imagine me, then, installed in his court at Poona, and flattered and envied as his chief favourite. Often my high position of power and influence turned my head, and I gloried to think that the life and death of the greatest nobles depended on my nod. When peace of mind and virtue were gone, power and the envy and admiration of others were my only consolations. But often I wept in secret at the loss of all that once was dear to me, and often I confess that I thought of the noble, fair-haired stranger who had braved the Peshwa's vengeance for my sake. But his name I never dared to mention, and should have had no inkling of his fate, had it not been for your interview with the Peshwa. It is now nearly a year since I was deposed from my proud position of reigning favourite in the Peshwa's zenana. A newer, perhaps a fairer, mistress has taken my place, and His Highness seldom speaks to me now except in terms of neglect. I happened to see him immediately after your departure to the British encampment, and asked him some trivial question, not noticing the cloud on his brow. 'Go out of my sight!' he exclaimed in words that cut me to my heart; 'you remind me of how, on your account, I was insulted by that vile Feringhi in your native village of Chinchwad. But thanks be to the immortal gods, I have him immured in my deepest dungeon, where he shall now perish of starvation, and his friend, who dared to mention his name in my presence, shall be sent to join him there when I have driven the accursed Feringhis far from my capital.'

"I went away half-stunned with his cruel words, and overcome with poignant sorrow on account of the evil that I had brought upon the head of my gallant defender, for whose welfare I have often prayed. This morning a messenger came to me telling me that the Peshwa had repented of his unkindness, that I might regain his favour if, without question, I would go to the Hirwa Bungalow to-morrow morning and there act as I should be ordered to act. They also told me that by so doing I should win myself a name for ever as one who had done good service to my country and my country's gods. The idea of action of any sort promised to gratify my craving for excitement, and the motives urged upon me were not without their effect on my mind. So I readily agreed to go to the bungalow. I have already told you how, owing to some change of plan, I was directed to go there this afternoon instead of to-morrow morning, and you yourself saw what followed.

"You have now heard all my miserable tale. Elphinstone Sahib offers to send me with honourable escort wherever I wish to go. I have long been disgusted with the fearful licence and gaudy glitter and wickedness of the Peshwa's court, and will never return to it. My soul yearns to return to a better life. To my father's house I can return no more. It is my fixed resolve to give up all my worldly possessions and worldly desires, and to become a jogin.[1] I have an aunt who is famous far and wide for her sanctity. She is a servant of the great god Mahadev, in his temple in Chauk, a village in the Konkan. There then I will go and assume the orange robe of the ascetic, and under my aunt's guidance will devote myself for the rest of my life to pious meditation and the worship of the gods. If Elphinstone Sahib will provide me with a palanquin and trusty bearers to conduct me thither, I will ever remember him and you in my prayers."

Her wish was complied with, and I bade her farewell, adjuring her, if she ever could obtain from pilgrims to the shrine to which she was going, or from any other source, information as to the place in which my friend was imprisoned, to let me know. She willingly made this promise and went her way, and I saw her no more.

Soon after her departure dinner was announced, and, preceded by Mr. Elphinstone's chobdars,[2] we walked over to the dining bunga-

[1] jogin = female ascetic.

[2] Chobdars = attendants who go before princes and other men of high rank in India, bearing maces overlaid with silver.

low, situated by the side of the river. To reach it we went through a beautiful garden in which grew orange, lime, papaya, and fig trees, broad-leaved plantains, the sweet-scented guava, and the stately jambul, sometimes called the Indian plum-tree. From the windows of the dining-room we saw on the right, across the river Mutha, the temples and palaces of Poona, illuminated by the silver light of the moon. On the left was the Hindu burning-ground, the light of the fires of which was a gruesome accompaniment to our repast. I thought to myself that, while we were joyously quaffing our wine, there might be on the other side of the river, within a stone-throw of where we sat, an unhappy widow who, for no fault of her own, was about to suffer a cruel death in the flames of the funeral pyre. It was only with an effort that I could shake off this melancholy thought and take delight in the scholastic flavour that Mr. Elphinstone's learning gave to the conversation, whether the subject was literature, politics, sports, or the manners and customs of the people.

In the morning, before leaving the Sangam, I besought Mr. Elphinstone to accept the coat of mail which had saved my life from the daggers of the assassins in the Hirwa Bungalow, and which might, if donned by him, preserve a life far more valuable to his country. But he courteously declined my offer, quoting his favourite fatalistic proverb from Herodotus: *οὐ φρόντις Ἱπποκλείδῃ* (Hippocleides does not care).[1] He explained to me that he always did his best, and that, if that did not serve, he then, like Hippocleides at the marriage feast, resigned himself to the inevitable. I was inclined to argue with him that he was not doing his best for himself and his countrymen if he did not use all feasible means to ward off the danger of assassination, with which he was continually threatened. But I saw that his Greek maxim in this case was only a courteous way of refusing to arm himself against danger at the risk of another, however insignificant that other might be.

[1] See Appendix, note 6.

CHAPTER XVII

BEFORE THE BATTLE

ONE of the most striking features in the beautiful landscape presented to the spectator who views Poona from the neighbourhood of the Sangam is the temple-crowned hill of Parvati, a few hundred yards to the south-east of the city limits, which rises like a Greek acropolis to a height of two hundred and sixty feet above the road to Sinhgad. From its top may be seen a fine view of Poona and the surrounding country, including the mountain fortresses of Sinhgad and Torna, with all their historic memories, and many another famous Maratha stronghold in the farther distance.

About four o'clock on the afternoon of Wednesday, Nov. 5, the Peshwa stood gazing out of a window on the northern face of the summit of Parvati. He looked over his capital towards the British encampment at Kirki and the ground between, over which his troops were moving in all the splendour of Oriental war. For at last he had conquered his irresolution and given the fateful word of command that Gokhle and his host should overwhelm the British force, that the Residency should be destroyed, and that all the British in Poona should be killed except Dr. Coats, to whose medical skill he had once been indebted for his life.

Still his mind was ill at ease. He was superstitious, and his mood was depressed by an evil omen. For when he had summoned his captains around him and raised the Juree Patka, or Golden Streamer, the national standard under which the Maratha chivalry had so often charged on to victory, the staff broke in the middle and the rich texture of the flag was defiled with dust. Also he was painfully conscious of the fact that at this great crisis of his own fate and of the national destiny he, the Peshwa, ought to be marshalling his soldiers sword in hand. For well he knew how much depended on the battle about to take place. If only his army could destroy the small British force at Kirki, he might hope that the whole Maratha nation would no longer hesitate between rival leaders, but rally round the Peshwa as the centre of national unity. If thus the rivalry and conflicts between himself, Scindia, and Holkar, and the other great Maratha chiefs could be brought to an end, the Marathas would not only drive the few British into the sea, but become conquerors of the whole of India from the Himalayas to Cape Comorin. A glorious future, as the Saviour of Maharashtra and the Emperor of India, awaited him, if only he could be himself the hero of the day, and, like Shivaji, or his own warlike ancestors, lead his soldiers to victory. Shame at his own pusillanimity almost overcame his constitutional timidity, and once he started up and exclaimed to those around him:

"The proper place for the Peshwa on such a day as this is at the head of his troops. Ho, Gokhle!" he said, turning to Govindrao, the captain of his body-guard, who, though burning with ardour to join in the battle, was detained by his side, "gird on my sword and order my horse to be got ready, and you and I will join your brave father."

For a moment his gallant bearing deceived them. Govindrao Gokhle eagerly picked up his master's diamond-hilted sword, a weapon more fitted for the show of state pageantry than for the stern work of battle, from the carpet on which it lay. And then a sudden shot was heard, and the wretched monarch trembled visibly like an aspen leaf. His courtiers were quick to see the change, and urged him not to risk his precious life to the chances of war.

"What good, oh Shrimant," one of them said, "is the body without the head? If a random bullet laid you low, the Marathas would be like sheep without a shepherd."

He was only too eager to take such advice, and allowed his sword to be replaced on the carpet at his feet.

Presently he began to repent that he had ordered Gokhle to attack the British, as he contemplated the disastrous consequences that would be the result of defeat. His irresolution soon rose to such a pitch that he called young Gokhle again to him and said:

"Ride quickly to your father and tell him that on no account is he to fire the first shot."

So Gokhle mounted his horse and rode towards Kirki. At first he did not ride very fast, as he was unwilling to bear such a message, and hoped that battle would be joined ere he could reach his father. But when he had crossed the wooden bridge over the River Mutha, and was in the open country, a sudden thought struck him, and, putting spurs to his horse, he galloped at full speed towards the head-quarters of the Maratha army. He had determined to tell his father that the Peshwa's orders were that he should hurry on the attack lest any of the defeated enemy should escape in the darkness of the night. By this lie he thought he should save his master the Peshwa from being disgraced for all time on account of his timidity and irresolution, and at the same time hasten the glorious victory that would make him at once the undisputed Monarch of Maharashtra and, in the future, Emperor of India. His own heart bounded with exultation at the prospect of taking part in the glorious fray.

Soon after he rode up to his father's station under the Golden Streamer, the whole Maratha army, consisting of some twenty-five thousand cavalry and as many infantry, moved forward to take up their position in the valley between Ganesh Khind and the River Mula. Their advance was the grandest spectacle that I have ever witnessed. The historian of the Marathas,[1]

[1] Captain Grant Duff, author of the *History of the Mahrattas.*

who saw it all from a commanding position on the hill above the powder-magazine at Kirki, has given a picturesque description of it all which my feeble pen cannot hope to emulate. "Those only", he writes, "who have witnessed the Bore in the Gulf of Cambay, and have seen in perfection the approach of that roaring tide, can form the exact idea presented to the author at sight of the Peshwa's army. It was towards the afternoon of a very sultry day; there was a dead calm, and no sound was heard except the rushing, the trampling and neighing of horses and the rumbling of the gun-wheels. The effect was heightened by seeing the peaceful peasantry flying from their work in the fields, the bullocks breaking from their yokes, the wild antelopes, startled from sleep, bounding off and then turning for a moment to gaze on this tremendous inundation, which swept all before it, levelled the hedges and standing corn, and completely overwhelmed every ordinary barrier as it moved."

To meet this seemingly irresistible advance, Colonel Burr, colonel of the 7th Regiment of Native Infantry and commander of the British forces at Poona, led out his little force of less than three thousand men, including the Bombay European Regiment in which I had obtained my commission. For, in accordance with Mr. Elphinstone's instructions, when open war was declared we were not to remain on the defensive, but were to march forward and attack the enemy. This order was well justified, not only by the general conditions of Oriental warfare, but also by the special circumstances of the case. The whole of British-Indian history shows clearly that in the East the best quality in strategy and tactics is "l'audace, l'audace, et toujours l'audace". Even the transfer of our headquarters from Garpir to the suburb of Kirki had given dangerous encouragement to Maratha presumption, and it was necessary to restore our prestige by assuming a bold bearing. Also, if we remained on the defensive there was more and more danger of our sepoys being seduced by the immense bribes offered to tempt them to be unfaithful to their salt. So we did well to advance in order of battle towards Ganesh Khind.

Before the opposing forces came into collision, we were joined on our right by Major Ford and his battalion from Dapuri, and on our left by Mr. Elphinstone and his escort of five hundred men, who had evacuated the Residency, and, fording the river, come round to Kirki by Holkar's Bridge. They had no time to take away anything with them except the clothes on their backs, and when, by the Peshwa's express orders, the bungalow was burnt, Mr. Elphinstone's valuable library and manuscripts perished in the flames.

CHAPTER XVIII

BATTLE OF KIRKI

THE battle was opened on the Maratha side by a sudden discharge from a battery of nine guns against our troops, which by this time had advanced nearly two miles in the direction of Poona from their first position at Kirki. Immediately not only our front but our right and left wings were enveloped by surging masses of Maratha cavalry, so that our small army was like a promontory beaten on all sides but one by the waves of a tempestuous sea. Fortunately for us, the Maratha cavalry had outstripped, by the rapidity of their advance, the Maratha infantry except one strong battalion commanded by De Pinto, a Portuguese soldier of fortune. The Maratha horsemen, in all the bravery of their gaily coloured scarves and turbans, with pennons fluttering at their lance heads, and the rays of the setting sun flashing from their swords and cuirasses, were a gallant and awe-inspiring sight; but, although their squadrons seemed in continual motion, they did not charge home.

The first collision was with De Pinto's battalion of infantry, which threatened the 7th Native Infantry Regiment on our left wing. Our sepoys, in their ardour to engage this battalion and drive it off the field, advanced beyond their position in the line. They were successful in their gallant charge; but by their sudden rush forward they left a dangerous gap between themselves and our European regiment in the centre of the line. The weak point did not escape the eyes of the commanders of the two opposed armies. Bapu Gokhle was on our left, with the flower of the Maratha chivalry arrayed round the Golden Streamer. I saw him, with drawn sword, leading his followers gallantly to charge into the gap and break our line in two. When his horse was shot under him, and he was thrown to the ground, his son and other chiefs who understood his intention charged on as boldly as before.

At this point of the battle the victory trembled in the balance. If once this great body of cavalry could have interposed itself between the sepoys of the 7th Native Infantry and the European regiment, we should probably, surrounded as we were on all sides, have been cut to pieces. We were saved partly by favour of the ground and partly by the coolness of Colonel Burr and the steadiness of the sepoy regiment, which showed good evidence of its discipline and loyalty. It happened, more by luck than good guidance, that our left wing was defended by a morass unknown both to ourselves and the enemy. Into this morass the foremost of the Maratha horsemen floundered, and, owing to the delay thus caused, those who managed to struggle through, found us ready to give them a warm reception when they came within striking distance. For in the meantime old Colonel Burr, having quickly grasped the situation, had called back the victorious sepoys from the pursuit of De Pinto's battalion. Like the well-trained soldiers that they were, they responded to their commander's call and returned to their place in the line. At the same time our Old Toughs moved forward gallantly to their support. Thus the imminent danger was averted, and the Maratha cavalry could make no impression. After one or two ineffectual charges, in which they suffered terribly from our fire, they gave up the attempt to break us and rode away. Among the very last to retire was young Gokhle, who had been foremost in every charge. I could sympathize with his feelings when I saw him at last compelled to retire and rejoin the great army of his countrymen, which had advanced with such gallant show and with such confidence in their power of easily achieving the victory.

For myself, I need not give an account of my feelings and experiences in my first battle. It was not a Homeric combat in which single captains crossed swords with one another. It was indeed a triumph of union and discipline over numbers. As far as individual glory was won, the honours of the day belonged to Mr. Elphinstone and Colonel Burr, who had planned the arrangements for the battle and carried them out so well, and to Bapu Gokhle, the Maratha general, who was so quick to see the chance of victory offered by the excessive ardour of the sepoy regiment. The fame of the defeated Maratha general is still celebrated in Maratha ballads,[1] because he so gallantly on that disastrous day, by personal

[1] See Appendix, note 7.

valour and by generalship, upheld his master's throne and maintained the warlike reputation of his country, when so many of his boastful followers fled without striking a blow for honour and freedom. It is enough for me that I shared with every sepoy and British soldier present the glory of that decisive victory won against an enemy that outnumbered us by more than twelve to one. It may well be called a decisive victory, although it was won with the loss of only eighty-six men in killed and wounded, and even the Maratha casualties only amounted to some five hundred men; for this battle was the deathblow to Maratha power. Never again had the Marathas a chance of regaining their position as the paramount power in India. The war, which was henceforth concerned with the capture of chiefly the hill fortresses of the Dekhan and the pursuit of the flying Peshwa and his army, dragged on until June, 1818, when Baji Rao surrendered to Sir John Malcolm, and almost all his wide dominions were added to the British Indian Empire.

CHAPTER XIX

HAIBATI SUMMONS ME TO BHOSARI

THIS being not a history of the last Maratha war, but a personal narrative, it is not necessary for me to give a detailed account of the military events that took place in Poona and the neighbourhood after the battle of Kirki. The Peshwa, although his numerical superiority had not been materially diminished by his defeat, did not venture again to take the offensive. On the 13th of November, General Smith, in command of the fourth division of the Dekhan army, joined us, and on the 15th our combined forces prepared to attack the Maratha army in Poona. On the 15th and 16th the Bombay regiment took part in the fighting at Yerowda Ford, and lost nineteen men in killed and wounded. After the ford was forced, the Peshwa and his army abandoned Poona and fled towards Satara, pursued by General Smith.

On the day following our reoccupation of

the old British encampment at Garpir, a native came to my tent, and, bending his forehead to the dust, showed me the gold stud that I had given as a token to Haibati at Kirki, when our interview was interrupted by the appearance of two Maratha horsemen. After he had gone through enough of humble obeisances, he informed me that the sender of the token awaited my coming at a place called Bhosari, on the Nasik road, eight miles north of Poona. If I would mount my horse, my humble suppliant, as the messenger called himself, would guide me there with all speed.

To go or not to go was a very difficult question to decide. On the one hand, the man who invited me to a conference had already betrayed me, and might do so again. On the other hand, from what I knew of the man, he was not likely to attach himself to the losing side. As he had himself pointed out at our last interview, he had been to England and could form a correct idea of British power; and, since we had met, the Peshwa's army had been defeated and the Peshwa had fled from his capital. But, after all, on such occasions one's action depends more upon feeling than upon reason and prudential regard for one's self-preservation. The great object of my desire was to win the hand of Alice Hannay and free her brother from captivity, and I was eager to adopt any means, however dangerous, that would promote that end. So I determined to go.

When I informed Major Wilson of my intention of going for a ride on the high ground on the other side of the river, he said:

"Better not go alone. Take warning from what happened to you when you rode alone from Kirki to Poona a fortnight ago."

I pointed out that since then the Marathas had been defeated and completely cowed, and that there was little likelihood of an British officer being molested.

"Very well," said he, "go your way, if go you must; but if what happened to yourself is not enough warning, remember how Captain Vaughan and his brother were murdered at Talegaon."

However, I had made up my mind, and, as Major Wilson did not care to exert his authority, as my superior officer, to keep me in camp, I mounted my horse Moti, which young Gokhle had given me, and followed my guide along the Nasik road. He girded up his loins and ran so swiftly, using the tail of my horse as a towing-rope, that in little more than an hour we reached our destination.

Haibati's stout figure was again disguised in the inappropriate garb of an ascetic. He was seated in an enclosure full of stones that had been erected to commemorate the valiant deeds done by forgotten warriors many centuries ago. His back rested against a standing stone that reminded me of those that are to be seen in the wild moorland between Gatehouse and Creetown, and in other parts of Galloway. Without rising from his seat, he touched his forehead with his hand and began:

"Was not I right in thinking that the Marathas could not resist the power of the Topiwalas?[1] Has not the strongest army of the Peshwas been driven from the field by a handful of British soldiers and their sepoys? A blind man might see on which side the gods are fighting. But I did not summon the sahib to come eight miles to hear what he knows already. I have news to tell you.

[1] Topiwalas = wearers of helmet, the British, who are distinguished from natives of India by wearing sun helmets.

But first swear that you will keep the promise you made to me at Kirki."

"What," I asked, "is the good of swearing again that I will keep an oath I have sworn already. If I could break one oath, I can break another. Tell me your news, and beware you do not deceive me, or you will rue it to your dying day!"

The tone in which I spoke thoroughly frightened him. He knelt down on the ground at my feet and besought me to forgive him.

"The sahib," he said, "is my father and my mother, and I am a poor man who have no other protector. Listen and I will tell you all. Your friend is imprisoned in the fort of Prabul."

"Where is Prabul?" I asked.

"When you marched here from Bombay," he replied, "twelve miles after leaving Panwell, you passed through the village of Chauk. Perhaps you noticed on your left two great mountains rising from the plain, with forests on their flat tops. Of these two mountains the larger one on the east is Matheran, and the smaller one towards Bombay and the setting sun is Prabul."

"How was it," I asked, "that the Peshwa chose a fort so near British territory as a place of confinement for a British officer?"

"This made me wonder also," he replied. "But I was told that the Peshwa, when he sent the captive to Prabul, said: 'Imprison him on the west side of the mountain, and let his cell have a window from which he can see Bombay, that he may look at the ships of Europe in the harbour, and be tortured by the thought that his friends are so near, and yet that it is impossible for him to reach them'."

On hearing this I marvelled at the refined cruelty that had dictated the Peshwa's choice of a prison for my friend, and thought of the misery John Hannay must have endured, month after month, looking through the window at the white houses of Bombay and the black hulls of the ships riding at anchor in the harbour. It was such a punishment as was devised for Tantalus in the infernal regions of Greek mythology.

My reflections on the sufferings of my friend were at this point interrupted by the arrival on the scene of a body of horsemen, who surrounded Haibati and me in such a way that escape was impossible. Four or five of them leapt from their horses, and, closing round us, called upon us to surrender. I drew my sword and attempted to defend myself. The foremost of my assailants bit the dust at my feet, but this did not check the onrush of the others, who soon wrenched my sword from my hand and bound me tight with thongs. Haibati attempted no resistance, and so escaped the rough treatment to which I was subjected.

CHAPTER XX

A CAPTIVE IN THE HANDS OF THE PINDARRIES

I SUPPOSED at first that my captors were a wandering band of the Maratha army. But they spoke to me in a language which was so different from Maratha that I could not understand much of what they were saying. So they put their questions to Haibati, and even he had some difficulty in conversing with them.

Their questions were mostly about the military situation, in which they appeared to be keenly interested. They had heard of Gokhle's repulse at Kirki, but now learnt for the first time that the British had occupied Poona, and that the Peshwa had fled. This intelligence appeared to be very unwelcome to them. Their leaders held a hurried consultation, the result of which was that they all leapt on their horses and prepared for a hurried departure. They mounted me on my own horse and put Haibati on the back of a good pony that they found in the nearest stable. One of the troopers rode beside each of us. As I was completely disarmed, and tied fast with a thong to the trooper who had charge of me, I saw little chance of escape, especially as we were always kept carefully in the middle of the party. In this manner we rode quickly for several miles along the Nasik road, away from Poona, until the sun set and the darkness compelled us to halt for the night by the roadside under a clump of great mango-trees.

The bivouac was extremely picturesque, and, in spite of the possibility of my captors deciding at any moment to kill me, I managed somehow to enjoy the scene. I could not help thinking what an effective picture my mother could have made of it, had she had an opportunity of painting the strange figures of the dusky troopers, moving among the trees or reclining gracefully on the turf. There was plenty of the charm of variety in their faces, dress, and accoutrements. Every caste was represented in the troop, from the haughty Brahmin, with clear olive complexion, high forehead, high-bridged nose,

B 392

A CAPTIVE

and curling upper lip, to the ugly little black-faced Bhil. A few of them were dressed in scarves of costly silk; some were wrapt in women's saris. Some of their turbans were interwoven with ornamental gold and silver thread, and showed as much variety of colour as constant exposure to the weather allowed them to retain. They had straight swords, crooked swords, short swords, and long swords, and many of them had, sticking in their belts, thick heavy pistols of a primeval pattern that might on occasion be used as short clubs in a hand-to-hand combat. There was the same variety in their horses. One or two were beautiful Arabs that might have been the glory of a prince's stud. Others were small country-breds, not beautiful to look at, but sure-footed and capable of any amount of hard work. They were tethered with heel-ropes, according to the Indian fashion, and neighed impatiently for their evening feed of grain. Above, among the branches of the trees on which they had been hanging head downwards by their hooked wings in sweet slumber, great flying-foxes flitted about, and by discordant cries manifested their indignation at the unwonted intrusion on their haunts. The whole scene was lit up here and there by the watch-fires, whose light was reflected from the weapons of the troopers as they walked about attending to their horses or cooking their frugal supper.

Our captors showed that they were not devoid of human kindness by providing Haibati and me with a fire to warm ourselves by, and one young man, with a rich gold ear-ring in his ear, threw over me a horse-cloth of red flannel, so that I might not suffer from the night dews.

When we were left alone, I asked Haibati who they were. He told me, to my horror and alarm, that they were a band of Pindarries, a fragment of one of those great marauding armies, to check whose wide-spread ravages Lord Hastings had gathered together the largest British army that ever took the field in India. This particular band, it appeared, had come into the neighbourhood of Poona, not for plunder, but to concert united action against the British between the Peshwa and the notorious Chitu, to whose army they belonged. The news of the Peshwa's flight southward from Poona had rendered their mission abortive and their position near Poona dangerous in the extreme, and this was the reason why they had beat a retreat so hastily from Bhosari after hearing the news from Haibati.

I shuddered when I thought of the terrible tales I had heard of the atrocities that had been committed by these marauders, not only on men, but also on weak women and children; how they ravaged the lands of the poor cultivators and extorted money from the rich by thrusting their heads into horses' nose-bags filled with red-hot ashes, and by setting fire to their clothes, which were smeared with oil to make them burn better. It was difficult to imagine that the kindly young man with the ear-rings, in whose horse-cloth I was then cosily wrapped, had taken part in such deeds, and might, perhaps, join the others in treating me in the same way if they thought there was any chance of thereby getting a larger ransom out of me.

I asked Haibati what he supposed they would do with us. He had told them that I was an officer of the British army, and if any harm were done to me or my servant, (for so Haibati chose to describe himself for the nonce), he warned them that the arm of the British Government was very long, and would terribly avenge us. Unfortunately he added that I was the nephew of a rich merchant in Bombay. The marauders had pricked up their ears at this intelligence. If, they said, I had a rich uncle, he would no doubt be willing to pay heavily for my safety. They hoped to find in this way a remedy for their desperate fortunes. They were shrewd enough to see that the Peshwa's defeat was a death-blow to the Pindarries, that the robber hordes of Karim Khan, Chitu, and Wasil Muhammad could not, without Maratha support, long resist the large British forces operating against them, and that the Pindarries would be hunted to death until they were utterly exterminated. So our captors determined to start business as plunderers on their own account, and make as much as they could for themselves out of my capture. In order to be in a position to get my ransom more conveniently, they were going to move in the direction of the town of Thana, twenty-four miles from Bombay, which was then the outpost of the narrow Bombay domain. This bold course was perhaps the least dangerous they could adopt.

In that part of Western India they were at the time least likely to meet with British troops, as all the available forces from Bombay would be moving south in pursuit of the Peshwa, and the main British armies were attacking the Pindarries two or three hundred miles to the north, in the valley of the Nerbudda.

CHAPTER XXI

MY CAPTORS BECOME MY FOLLOWERS

EARLY next morning, before the first dim streak of gray in the east was tinged with red, we resumed our journey. Avoiding the main road between Bombay and Poona through the Bhor Ghaut, we made for the Bhimashankar Ghaut, the next passage down to the lowlands of the Konkan. In the afternoon, wearied with our long ride, we arrived at the village of Bhimashankar, where is the source of the River Bhima. A tiny stream trickles into a cistern, whence the waters flow eastward for a thousand miles till they mingle with the waters of the Bay of Bengal. So sacred is the source of the great river that it is supposed to cure diseases and wash away the guilt of sin. So the Pindarries were eager to bathe in the cistern, and Haibati, whose belief in the superstitions of his native land a visit to Europe had not entirely extinguished, did likewise.

I was given my evening meal of milk and

cakes made of the grain called bajri, coarse food which, thanks to my long ride through the keen air of the Dekhan, I was able to eat with a certain amount of relish. My seat, as I took my repast, was on the edge of the mountain, and commanded a splendid prospect of the Konkan plain, spread out below me like a map. The central point of the view was the great mountain of Matheran, behind which the sun was setting. It was less than twenty miles distant, and immediately behind it, but hidden from my eyes, was the mountain of Prabul, on which, as I had heard from Haibati, my friend was confined. As I looked, how my soul longed, in the words of Horace, "spatiis obstantia rumpere claustra"! Had I not been a captive, how swiftly would I have hurried to his release!

As I was thinking thus, an idea flashed into my mind which made me start up from the ground, forgetful of my captive state. The men who had been told off to watch me sprang upon me and held me fast, fearing that I contemplated rushing violently down the cliff to certain destruction. However, I soon managed to convince them by my quiescence that I had no such intention, and partly by words, partly by signs, asked them to allow Haibati to come to me. They acceded to my request, and brought Haibati, whom I asked to invite the leader of the Pindarries to come to a conference with me on a matter that much concerned them.

It appeared that they had no one recognized leader, for three of them came in answer to my invitation, and none of the three claimed superiority over the other two, although one of them acted as spokesman throughout the interview.

"May I ask," I began, "what advantage you expect to derive from my capture? Is it a light thing to incur the wrath of the great Government that has driven the Peshwa out of Poona, and at the same time is chasing your robber armies from one refuge to another?"

"We know well the power of the British," they replied; "but we are already their enemies, and if we fall into their hands may expect no mercy, except such as we may extort from them by having a hostage, whom we may kill. But know that we expect to escape them, and carry away with us the large ransom they will pay for your safety."

"And how," I said, "can you hope to get that ransom without approaching dangerously near a British army, or Bombay the centre of British power?"

"All the British regiments," he replied, "have gone far south to pursue the Peshwa, or northward to war against the Pindarries. There can be none left near Bombay, and we can safely lie in hiding somewhere, and wait till the ransom is paid."

"The British Government," I replied, "will never pay a rupee to a band of robbers with arms in their hands."

"If they won't, your uncle will, who, as we have heard, is the richest merchant in India."

"What ransom do you propose to demand?"

"The least we can ask from such a rich man," he said, "is a thousand rupees."

"What guarantee could you give my uncle that, after receiving one thousand rupees, you would deliver me up, and not immediately demand another thousand rupees? You could hardly expect him to trust your verbal promise. You may be all men of honour, my friends, but you are utter strangers to him, and he could scarcely be expected to trust you."

This was rather a poser for them. They talked together in whispers, but did not appear able to arrive at a solution of the difficulty. I took advantage of their hesitation as a good opportunity to introduce my proposal.

"If you wish," I said, "to escape from the evils by which you are surrounded, throw yourselves on the mercy of the British Government. Earn a rightful claim to their favour by restoring me unharmed, and you will never repent of your action. Further, if, as I think, you are men of mettle, you may do more. Besides restoring me, whom you have captured, you may release another British officer, who is in the hands of the Marathas, not twenty miles from here. If you do this double service to the British Government, you will be able to choose your own reward. Should you prefer the life of soldiers, you may enlist in the Company's army, where you will get good pay and a pension in your old age. If you are weary of strife, you will be given land in British territory, which you can cultivate without fear of the spoiler. Over and above all the favour that the British Government will give you, I promise each man of you fifty rupees if you set free my friend from his captivity."

"You tell us that your uncle could not trust our word. Tell us now why we should trust your solemn promise. How do we know that you will not, as soon as you are safe back in the middle of your sepoys, get rid of all your obligations to us by hanging us all to the highest tree?"

"Ask Haibati here," I replied. "He knows something about the way in which the British Government keeps its promises. He will tell you how the sepoys, though tempted with great bribes by the Peshwa, were faithful to their salt, and preferred their pay and the certainty of pension in the British service to the splendid promises made by the Peshwa's agents. Ask him also whether he thinks that I am a man likely to prove ungrateful and false to my promise."

Haibati supported me by giving a long dissertation on the power and justice of the British Government, and told them that he himself had, absolutely relying on my promise, braved the vengeance of the Peshwa, and had done so when he was a mighty monarch and not, as now, a fugitive."

"Well," replied the Pindarrie, "we will go and think over what you have said. If we agree to your proposal, we can keep Haibati in our hands as a hostage. By agreeing to this he will show in deed that he really trusts your word."

This conversation took a good long time, as the Pindarrie spokesman did not reply to any of my remarks without a whispered consultation with his colleagues. When it was over, they retired to submit my proposals to their followers before giving their final answer.

I derived hope from the fact that, while this council was being held, I was released from my bonds, and allowed, under the guidance of a priest, to visit the sacred places of Bhimashankar. As it was now quite dark, we had to be lighted on our way by torches. Close by the holy tank there were two temples, a new one recently completed by the wife of Nana Fadnavis, the famous Maratha minister, and an old one, the origin of which was shrouded in the mist of antiquity. According to the story told me, many centuries ago a Hindu labourer was cutting trees on its site, when, like Æneas in the third book[1] of the

[1] See Appendix, note 8.

Æneid, he saw blood oozing from the gash. The gruesome mystery was explained by the sudden appearance of the great god Mahadev, in whose honour the wood-cutter built a shrine.

The temple was built of dark stone, almost destitute of ornamentation, except the pendants supplied by nature in the form of stalactites dripping from the eaves. Under the centre of the vaulted dome was an image, in rough stone, of Nundi, the bull ridden by Mahadev, and by the dim, religious light of a hanging lamp I could see a priest offering fresh flowers to the god. To the east of this old temple, in strange juxtaposition with its heathen images, was a Christian relic, a bell inscribed with a representation of the Virgin Mary, a cross, and the date 1729. It had probably been left there by the Marathas returning from the capture of the great Portuguese city of Bassein in 1739. The red paint smeared over the figure and on the cross showed that the bell was, in its strange position, an object of adoration to the Hindu worshippers at the temple.

While I was visiting the temples, the Pindarries had concluded their council by taking Haibati under a sacred fig-tree, among the rustling leaves of which the gods are believed to sit. There, in the hearing of the gods supposed to be immediately above him, he had to take a leaf in his hand, and, crushing it, pray the gods so to crush him and all near and dear to him if what he had said about me and the British Government was untrue. He went through the ordeal successfully, and came to me with the whole band of Pindarries, about a hundred strong, just as I returned from my torchlight walk.

They told me that, threatened as they were by dangers on every side, they could not refuse my offer, and accepted me as their leader and protector. They only stipulated that, as long as they remained under my command and served me faithfully, they should receive pay at the rate of ten rupees a month, and that if any of them were killed in the enterprise against Prabul, the sum of fifty rupees due to him should be paid to his wife and children. I willingly agreed to these additional terms, especially to the latter, which showed that their wild and lawless life had not destroyed in their hearts the instincts of natural affection.

CHAPTER XXII

BHIMASHANKAR TO PRABUL

THUS by a freak of fortune, instead of being a helpless captive in the hands of men notorious for their cruelty, I had myself become captain of a band of robbers, but of robbers who had sworn to take part in an honourable enterprise, and whom I had every hope of converting from their evil life and transforming into faithful soldiers in the British Indian army. My first command to them was that they should choose officers. They accordingly assembled together, and by a rough form of popular election selected the three men who had been their representatives in the recent conference with me, and the young man with gold ear-rings, who had so kindly lent me a horse-cloth to defend me against the cold.

Next morning we had another early start. We descended the pass by a long winding path practicable for bullock-carts. During a large portion of our way the great masses of trap rock on which Tungi fort is built towered above us. The Maratha garrison might have done us much damage as we passed, by merely rolling down stones on our heads; but we slipped along quietly, concealing ourselves as much as possible from view, and if we were noticed, the Marathas had no means of telling whether we were friends or foes. So our progress was unmolested, and we arrived without loss at the village of Kandas in the Konkan.

At Kandas, by making use of my uncle's name, which appeared to be well known throughout the country, I induced a native grain-dealer to give my troop a liberal supply of food. From what they told me, it must have been quite a novel experience for them to eat a meal the materials for which were not the product of robbery.

From Kandas we proceeded across the plain westward, in the direction of Matheran. If we had gone to the right of the mountain, we should have been in great danger of being observed and attacked by the Maratha garrison on the fortified hill of Peb, which lies just beyond the spur of Matheran, now known as Panorama Point. So we turned towards the west, and, passing along below Garbut and Chauk Points, made for the valley of the

Dhauri, the stream that flows between Matheran and Prabul, past the village of Chauk, into the Patalganga.

As we skirted round Chauk Point we kept to the high ground, and proceeded along the fine belt of forest which encircles Matheran half-way up, and is known to the frequenters of that hill station as the Ram Bagh, or Primeval Forest. By this course we gave a wide berth to the main road past Chauk village, and saw what was going on there while we were ourselves concealed by the forest trees.

Under the shade of the trees we halted for our mid-day rest, and I, with Haibati and one of my lieutenants, went up a high rock that commanded a view of the village of Chauk and the main road. What was our surprise to see that a large encampment had been established in and around the village! The confused medley of camels, elephants, horses, and men that we saw could not for a moment be mistaken for a British force. It was evidently a portion of the Maratha army, but it was difficult to form an estimate of its strength. It might be one, or two, or even three thousand strong.

We were not much wiser on the subject of

their number when we got hold of a Thakur who was gathering wood in the forest. He had been close to Chauk an hour or two before, but his power of counting was extremely limited. He confirmed, however, our conjecture that they were Marathas, and he had heard that they were a collection of all the Maratha soldiers that could be spared from the Konkan after leaving sufficient garrisons for Mahuli, Malanggad, and the other principal fortresses, and that they were going up the Bhor Ghaut with the intention of joining the Peshwa at Poona. He could not, however, tell us whether they were going up the Ghaut directly, or would wait a day or two until other bodies of Marathas from more distant parts of the Konkan should join them. Our informant knew Prabul well, and had often taken supplies of grain and fuel to the Marathas who held the fort. The garrison, he said, was a very small one, only amounting to about a hundred men. He did not know that they had any prisoners in their charge.

Such being the information at our disposal, it was difficult to decide what we ought to do. There were two courses open to us. We might remain without much fear of discovery in the Primeval Forest until the Marathas left Chauk, and then attack Prabul; or we might go there at once.

I was inclined to take the latter course for several reasons. We did not know how long we might have to wait for the departure of the Marathas. If John Hannay were in Prabul now, he might be taken away up to the Dekhan by the departing Marathas. Probably a large number of the garrison of Prabul would be down at Chauk to enjoy the society of their friends, and those few who remained on the mountain might easily be surprised and overpowered. But could we climb the mountain unperceived by the Marathas assembled at Chauk? And, if we found it necessary, was there any path on the other side by which we could escape pursuit? We questioned the Thakur woodcutter on these points and received satisfactory answers. He knew every inch of the ground, and would conduct us across the valley of the Dhauri to Prabul by a roundabout route so overshadowed by trees that those going by it would be invisible to spectators from Chauk. There were also, he said, several paths by which we could descend the other side of the mountain.

This information decided me to take immediately the action which I myself had previously been inclined to take. So, after a sufficient rest, we started under the woodcutter's guidance, keeping to the shelter of the Primeval Forest. We passed the foot of the rocky staircase known as Jacob's Ladder, and then struck across the valley in the direction of the centre of Prabul.

CHAPTER XXIII

ASCENT OF PRABUL

PRABUL is over two thousand feet high, about the height of the Cairnsmoors, three of the highest mountains in the southern highlands of Galloway. It was no light matter to climb it in the tropics, with the prospect of an enemy to fight us when we reached the top. Before commencing the ascent we had to weaken our strength by leaving twenty men at the foot of the mountain in charge of the horses, which they were to take round to the western side of the mountain as soon as they knew that we were firmly established on the top. For if all went well, and we succeeded in effecting John Hannay's release from captivity, we were to descend to the plain on the Bombay, that is the western, side of Prabul, and make our way as quickly as possible to British territory.

The first part of the ascent was by a narrow path, through thick jungle that obstructed every breath of air. When we had struggled half-way up the hill, we turned to the right, and found ourselves in the rocky bed of a mountain stream, at the top of a mighty precipice, over which the water falls down a sheer drop of eight or nine hundred feet. Hives of bees swarming on the edge of the rock appeared to have been recently robbed of their honey, for there were numbers of them buzzing about in a wild state of commotion at the top of the cliff. The Thakur, who was guiding us, knew well how dangerous these insects were when irritated. He implored me to tell my men to go as quietly as possible past them, so as not to turn their fury on ourselves. So we clambered up the rocky boulders as silently as a chorus of conspirators in the opera, but, even so, did not escape without a sting or two. The river-bed was very rough, and we had often to clamber up it on hands and feet. At last we were nearly at the top of the mountain, and saw immediately above us the wall of the fortress.

As far as we could see, peering carefully from behind the rocks and trees that shrouded us, there was not even a sentry on the wall. The garrison might, however, be behind it, reserving their fire to deliver a deadly volley when we came close up. So one or two of our men went forward as scouts. They saw

B 592

"AT LAST WE SAW ABOVE US THE WALL OF THE FORTRESS"

no signs of the presence of any defenders, and presently one of them ventured to climb the wall, and found no one on the ramparts. Soon after our scouts had brought us this welcome intelligence we all clambered up the wall and found ourselves within the fortifications of Prabul.

We had good reason to congratulate ourselves on our good fortune in effecting an entry into the fort without the loss of a man, and without any more severe wounds than those inflicted by the stings of two or three bees. The fort could at this point have been defended easily against great odds. As we stood on the wall and looked down, we entirely commanded the steep ascent, and the big loose stones collected for defensive purposes on the top of the wall seemed enough to demolish any assailants who might attempt to force their way up the rocky ravine.

Eager as I was to prosecute my quest, I delayed a moment on the ramparts to enjoy the view of the great mountain of Matheran, half-illumined by the light of the setting sun and half-shrouded by the shadow of Prabul. But what were these objects that we saw moving at the bottom of the ravine, just at the point where we had slipped past the bees? We watched them intently for a few moments, and soon made out that they were armed men. No doubt, in spite of all our precautions, we had been observed from the Maratha camp at Chauk as we crossed the valley between Matheran and Prabul, and a detachment had been sent after us to ascertain who we were and, if necessary, to attack us. As we watched them, one by one or by groups, emerging from the forest and creeping up the bed of the torrent, it was evident that the pursuing force far outnumbered us. In their excitement some of my men, without orders, rushed to the great stones collected at the top of the wall and began to push them over. I called out to them to stop and reserve their missiles till the enemy came nearer, but they did not hear, or would not obey me. The great stones fell crashing from the wall and hurtled down the ravine with bigger and bigger leaps and bounds, breaking the trees and raising powder-like smoke, when they fell on the rocks with a horrible grinding noise like the snarl of an angry wild beast.

The stones were soon in the middle of the Marathas, who crouched behind any obstacle that would shield them from their fury. Presently, when the torrent of great stones had passed by them and plunged into the forest beneath, our enemies emerged from their places of shelter; but, instead of resuming their ascent of the bed of the torrent, we saw them rushing madly to and fro, and in a way that must have endangered life and limb in such a rocky place. We were at a loss to understand what it all meant, until the Thakur, with a look of horror and alarm, whispered in my ear the Marathi word for "Bees".[1] The avalanche of stones, coming on the top of the irritation they had already been subjected to, had excited the bees to fury, so that they sallied forth in their myriads and attacked the unfortunate Marathas. Such an assault was irresistible. Our insect allies drove our enemies headlong down the mountain-side, stinging many of them to death, and maddening others with terror, so that they leapt to certain destruction over the precipice of rock from which the great waterfall descends in the centre of the eastern side of Prabul. Those who reached the foot of the mountain with unbroken limbs never halted till they reached the village of Chauk.

[1] See Appendix, note 9.

CHAPTER XXIV

JOHN HANNAY'S PRISON

IT was about the hour of sunset that, thanks to the diversion caused by our powerful little winged allies, we found ourselves seemingly undisputed masters of the eastern wall of Prabul. We did not, however, know whether the fort had been entirely evacuated by the garrison, or whether the wall we had scaled had been left undefended owing to the unlikelihood of an attack being made. The Thakur who had been our guide informed us that the dwelling-places of the garrison were some buildings at the southern end of the mountain. There, then, we might expect to find the captive and his jailers, if they had not descended to Chauk. There was no time to be lost. Night would soon be upon us, or, worse still, a second force might be despatched against us from the Maratha army at Chauk. So we turned to the left, and, with rapid steps, followed our guide, keeping a sharp look-out for the presence of an enemy as we advanced under the lengthening shadows.

Our path followed the edge of the mountain, from which we commanded a view of the valley of the Dhauri and the road leading from Chauk up the Ghauts. To my great satisfaction I saw, proceeding along the road in the direction of the Ghauts, large bodies of Marathas, dwarfed by distance to the size of ants. The whole army was evidently leaving Chauk, and we should, therefore, have little reason to fear another attack. But what if the Marathas were carrying off with them the prisoner whose recovery was the one object of all our exertions? Why, then, if that were the case, I was foiled for the present, and must try again. However, our doubts would soon be resolved, for we were now nearing the southern end of the mountain and the bastion, the sharp angle of which so often attracts the attention of the English visitor to Matheran hill station as he surveys Prabul from Landscape or Echo Point.

When we were close to the buildings, and had still descried no Maratha, we sent forward the Thakur to spy out the land before us. He crept forward through the brushwood as noiselessly as a snake gliding through the grass. After no long space of time he returned with the news that all the buildings were entirely empty. We were too late! The captive whom we sought to release, if he had ever been at Prabul, was evidently there no longer.

I was entirely at a loss what to do next. The only course open to us seemed to be to follow the Maratha army up the Ghauts in the hope that chance might afford us an opportunity of discovering and releasing my friend, if he was still a prisoner in their hands. In the meantime the darkness of night had enveloped the mountain. Exhausted nature required a rest, and we prepared to pass the night in the buildings recently evacuated by the Marathas.

Tired as I was, I could not lay myself down to sleep before I had examined the buildings, in one of which, as I had reason to believe, my friend had been imprisoned for many months. Few signs of human occupation were left behind. The walls of the rooms were of bare stone, and the floors were smeared, after the Indian fashion, with cow-dung. Only one building was two stories high. When I had mounted the solid stone staircase that led to the upper story, and told the torch-bearer to pass his torch along the walls, I immediately saw enough to convince me that Haibati's information had been true, and that he had not sent me on a wild-goose chase when he told me that my friend was imprisoned in the fort of Prabul.

My first glance at the walls of this upper chamber showed me that it had been John Hannay's prison. Certain scratchings on the east wall of the room, on being closely investigated, revealed themselves, even by the wavering light of the torch, to be a representation of Rusko Castle, with the River Fleet flowing below it. On the southern wall there was a still more interesting memorial of the prisoner. This was a diary, with the days of the month marked from the beginning of November, 1816, to November 19, 1817. How my heart beat with excitement on seeing these authentic records of my long-lost friend, and what a bitter grief it was that I had not arrived to succour him a day earlier! For "November 19", the last day marked on his diary, was the very day on the afternoon of which we had scaled the hill. However, there was also much material for comfort in what the torchlight revealed to my eyes. In the first place, it was evident that John Hannay, so long mourned as dead, had been alive and well that very day. I say "alive *and well*", because the figures in the diary were very distinctly engraved in the boulders of red laterite of which the walls were composed, and this could hardly have been done by a man in weak health, with a flint or big nail, or such blunt and imperfect implements as a prisoner could be safely trusted with. Also the diary and the representation of Rusko Castle, and the other pictures on a smaller scale that I found engraved on the walls when I examined them by the light of the morrow's rising sun, showed that he had found in his imprisonment an occupation to wile away the time, keep his spirits up, and prevent him from yielding to despair. It is true that he was still a prisoner, but the Marathas had on more than one occasion treated their British captives kindly, and were not in the habit of killing their prisoners in cold blood. At least I had never heard of any instance of their doing so. Even if I could not effect my friend's release more speedily, he would probably be restored safe and sound at the end of the war. Dwelling as much as possible on these comforting reflections, I managed to fall asleep and enjoy the rest that was so necessary to refresh me after the labours of that day, and to prepare me for whatever had to be done on the morrow.

CHAPTER XXV

MY LOST FRIEND FOUND

NEXT morning, before sunrise, my troop was ready for the march. We went down the path, past the southern bastion of the fort, towards the village of Chauk, my intention being to follow the track of the Maratha army towards Poona, or in whatever direction it might prove to be going. As we neared Chauk we descried a fine palanquin, with eight bearers, leaving the village in the direction of Panwell and Bombay. As soon as they saw it, some of my disorderly followers immediately, without waiting for orders, ran after the palanquin, hoping no doubt that anyone who could afford to travel so luxuriously would prove well worth plundering. I hurried after them to prevent any outrage being done to the unknown traveller.

When I arrived on the scene I found the bearers of the palanquin remonstrating with my men for molesting the noble lady whom they were carrying to Panwell.

"She is," they said, "of the Peshwa's court, and anyone who does her wrong will be severely punished."

"If she is of the Peshwa's court," replied the most audacious of my followers, "she is more likely to have rich jewels on her person. Let her hand them out and go in peace."

I gave the impudent fellow a blow across the back with the flat of my sword, and was proceeding, in the best Marathi at my command, to assure the supposed lady that she need fear no harm, when a hand drew aside the curtain of the palanquin, and stretched at full length on the cushions was revealed a strange figure, who exclaimed:

"Why, I do believe you are Aleck MacCulloch! Where in the world, or the sky, have you dropped from?"

I recognized him immediately in spite of the long yellow beard and the nondescript garments of unbleached cotton in which he was disguised. It was John Hannay.

We shook hands warmly, and exclaimed "By Jove!" once or twice, such being the strongest expression of joy and surprise that we unemotional northerners could bring ourselves to utter.

"And how are you, John," I said, "after your long imprisonment? You look rather stouter than when you left us. I don't think you have been suffering from starvation, fever, or any other disease."

"No, thank heaven!" he replied, "I am well and hearty, although you have found me riding like a fine lady in a palanquin. And I fear that for the present I cannot venture to put my foot on the ground, for I have sprained my ankle badly, and could neither walk nor ride."

"Such being the case you must remain in your travelling-bed, and, as we proceed along the road to Bombay, I will walk by your side and you must tell me the story of your captivity and escape."

"First," he said, "tell me about the dear ones I left in misty Galloway—my sister Alice, my father, your brother Tom, and your father and mother."

I told him that, though his father's health had suffered from grief and suspense about his fate, the good news of his safety would soon work a cure, and that all the others were well.

"Then," said he, "let me have something

to eat. For I am nearly famished, and, as that grim old jester, the lord of Threave,[1] once truly remarked to his guest: 'It is ill talking between a full man and a fasting'."

I might have told him that I was about as hungry as he was. However, my eagerness to hear his story prevented me from arguing the point. So I hastily gave him from our scanty stores some chapatties,[2] plantains, and milk, on which simple fare he made a most hearty meal, as we went on our way westward.

I was angry with my Pindarrie followers on account of their recent display of turbulence, and wished to be rid of them while I was listening to the story of my long-lost friend. So I sent them all away, rather rashly as the event showed. Three of them I sent on in front to the village of Panwell, twelve miles distant, to secure us comfortable accommodation there, and engage boats to convey us across the creek to Bombay. The rest I ordered to go back to join the twenty men who had been left at the foot of the western slope of Prabul with our horses, when we ascended the mountain. They were then to

[1] See Appendix, note 10.

[2] Chapatties = cakes resembling Scotch scones.

overtake us on our way to Panwell as speedily as they could, for I had had my fill of walking since the preceding afternoon, and longed once more to be mounted on the good horse that Govindrao Gokhle had given me at Poona.

CHAPTER XXVI

JOHN HANNAY'S STORY

"THE last letter that I wrote to my father", John Hannay began, "informed him that the 18th Hussars had been ordered to Poona. We arrived there in the middle of October, and naturally, after the tedium of a long and unexciting campaign, were disposed to plunge into all kinds of dissipation and extravagance and folly. The Peshwa and his nobles provided us with all kinds of entertainments on such a scale of magnificence as is only to be met with in the courts of Oriental princes with an unlimited supply of money at their command."

"Was Captain Moore with you?" I asked, "and what part did he take in these festivities?"

"Oh, you know my good cousin Captain Moore, do you?" he replied. "He was the leader of us all in every extravagance. From his horses and equipages, and the rich entertainments he gave to natives as well as Europeans, he might have been supposed to have an income of many thousands, instead of being an officer living on his pay supplemented by a small allowance from his friends at home."

"How do you account," I asked, "for his ability to make so much show on his small income?"

"It was a puzzle to me," John replied. "In our meetings with the Maratha nobles we had many gambling-matches. Captain Moore was a bold gambler, but, although he had extraordinary luck, the dice would not always fall in his favour, and he sometimes lost heavily. A day or two before the hunting expedition which led to my capture and imprisonment, I myself, at a gambling-bout, won from him at one sitting many thousand pounds."

"Did you, John Hannay," I asked in surprise, "take to gambling and at such a high rate?"

"The temptations were great," he replied, "and not easy to resist. I did my best to avoid gambling, and for some time succeeded. But, without taking part in this exciting amusement, life at Poona, with its native weddings and nautches, was unutterably dull. At first, and for a long time, I avoided high play. At last, on the night to which I referred, I was tempted to throw all my good resolutions to the wind. My rashness was owing to my having drunk rather more wine than I was accustomed to take. It was a small party, consisting of Captain Moore, myself, one or two officers from the Residency, and four of the richest Sirdars of the Dekhan. I began by venturing a large stake, far beyond my means, and won. Emboldened and excited by my success, I made a larger stake, and won again. All through the night, until the dawn appeared, I continued betting recklessly, and the dice appeared to be charmed in my favour. I won from all present at the party, especially from Captain Moore, who, when we parted at sunrise, owed me between six and seven thousand pounds. But your questions about Captain Moore have diverted me from the story of how I became a captive, to which I must now return."

"Perhaps Captain Moore and your captivity", I remarked, "may be more closely connected than you imagine. But go on."

"A day or two after the gambling-party

Captain Moore proposed that we should go tiger-shooting on the mountains of Mahableshwar. I readily agreed to the proposal, as I was utterly tired of Poona. The Oriental magnificence of the Peshwa's court had no attractions for me, and I had learnt that I was not able to resist the dangerous fascination of gambling. Besides, I had offended the Peshwa in a way that he was not likely to forget."

He then related how he had, at Chinchwad, defended an unknown Maratha lady against the licence of the Peshwa, and struck that proud prince on the face with his riding-whip.

"The Peshwa kept his affront buried in his bosom, and I could see in the countenances of his nobles no sign to indicate their knowledge of what I had done to their master, although they were never as familiar with me as they were with Moore. Yet, though neither the Peshwa nor his nobles showed any change of countenance when they met me, I knew that he had not failed to identify me as the insolent foreigner who had dared to brave him in his own dominions, and I was convinced that he was only waiting for a convenient opportunity for revenge. Events soon showed that my surmise was correct.

"Moore and I started on our shooting expedition. The shikari[1] met us at Wai and gave us news of the whereabouts of two large tigers, one of which was a man-eater. I was full of ardour, as this was the first chance I had had in India of encountering the monarch of the Indian jungle. Moore at first appeared to be equally eager; but once or twice, when I came upon him suddenly, he appeared to be distressed with melancholy. Supposing this might be due to the burden of his gambling debts, I told him that, of course, between friends and relations such as we were, there could be no idea of making money out of a friendly game, and that I had torn up all his I.O.U.'s. He answered angrily that he always paid his debts of honour, and left me in a fit of high dudgeon. I did not think much of the incident until half an hour afterwards, when I received a note informing me that after the insulting proposal that I had made to him he could accompany me no longer, and would return to Poona, leaving me the shikari in case I should choose to go on alone to

[1] Shikari = native hunter.

Mahableshwar. Since then I have seen him no more, but from conversation with some of my captors afterwards I learnt that on his return to Poona he became still more intimate with the Peshwa than before, to such an extent that he fell under the suspicion of the British Government.

"From Wai, accompanied by the shikari, I ascended two thousand feet higher, and found myself on the plateau of Mahableshwar. On the high ground that rises above the spur now known as Elphinstone Point we heard fresh tidings of the ravages of one of the tigers. A large cow had been killed and half-eaten. It was expected that the tiger, according to the practice of the animal, would return in the evening to devour the remainder of the carcass. So the usual arrangement was made to secure the safety of the hunter and the death of the tiger. A convenient seat was constructed for me on a tree overlooking the remains of the dead cow, and there I seated myself in the evening with my gun in my hand. The shikari occupied a similar seat on a neighbouring tree, with directions not to shoot until I had emptied my barrel. It seemed to me rather a cowardly method of meeting the tiger. As long as you stick to your seat on the tree, he has no chance of getting at you. However, chivalry is perhaps misplaced in contending with a wild beast. At any rate I took my seat on the tree, and awaited the tiger's approach without any serious qualms of conscience. The arrangement worked without a hitch. The tiger did not disappoint our expectations, but turned up at the expected time. I directed my aim at his striped body, dimly visible among the bushes by the light of the full moon, and the loud roar that followed showed that my shot had not failed to take effect. The beast, however, was only wounded, and, before I could reload, sprang at the tree on which I was sitting. He could not, however, jump as high as my perch, and fell back on the ground. At the same time a shot was heard from the shikari's gun, which, instead of hitting the tiger, struck the tree just above my head. Such a bad shot from a man with the shikari's reputation certainly surprised me. I reloaded my gun, and, cautiously descending, approached the tiger, which was still lying at the foot of the tree. He turned out to be quite dead. His spring at the tree had been made in his death-agony. I then went to look for the shikari, but he was nowhere to be found, and to this day I have never seen him again.

"I had now good reason to be seriously alarmed for my life. The disappearance of the shikari, after his very suspicious shot, made it probable that he had been hired to assassinate me. He might be lurking behind any of the trees, with the intention of repeating the attempt on my way back to camp. It was useless for me to attempt to save my life by going in a different direction, as we were far away from the main road, and the country was entirely unknown to me. So I retraced my steps to our encampment, imagining all the way that I saw the shadow of a man behind every tree, and every moment expecting to hear the report of a gun. As I proceeded in constant fear of my life, my mind was busied with conjectures as to the motive that had prompted the shikari to attempt my life. It seemed improbable that he should venture to do so for my gold watch and chain, and the chance of finding rupees in my pockets. My friend Moore and many others knew that he had gone out with me, and without the connivance of the Peshwa's officers he could not hope to escape the penalty of his crime. But how if he had been bribed to commit the crime, and promised protection, by one of the Peshwa's rich nobles who owed me considerable sums of money as the result of the recent gambling bout? Reckless as they were of the sanctity of human life, I could hardly think it worth their while to instigate murder to save themselves from the payment of sums of money which would, after all, not be any appreciable diminution of their rich incomes."

"Was there not another," I asked, "who had lost more heavily than the Maratha nobles, and who was far less likely to be able to pay his debts?"

"You surely do not mean to insinuate that a British officer and my cousin could have had any part in such a dastardly plot. You do yourself little honour, Aleck MacCulloch, by such base suspicions. Did he not also indignantly refuse remission of his debt when it was freely offered him?"

"You forget," I said, "that that offer was made to him after the time when the plot against you must have been formed. Perhaps if you had made the offer earlier, your life and liberty might never have been threatened.

But I am interrupting your story by suspicions of a brother officer which may be unjust, ungenerous, and unfounded. You were telling how you were returning to your camp, expecting every moment to hear what might be your death-shot."

"That death-shot never came," he said, "but long before I reached my camp some half-dozen men rushed upon me suddenly from under the deep shade of a clump of mango-trees. I fired at them as they advanced, but, owing to the suddenness of the attack and the uncertain light, I did not succeed in hitting any of them. In spite of all the resistance I could offer, they soon bound me with cords, put me in a palanquin that they had ready, and bore me through the night I knew not whither. Instead of curtains, the palanquin had wooden doors, which were tightly closed, so that I could not see out, and no curious passer-by should have a glimpse of its occupant. All that I could make out was that I was being carried rapidly downhill along a rough road often obstructed with bushes, which had occasionally to be cut out of our way by the swords or axes of those who had seized me. During my descent I again began to puzzle over the explanation of the treatment I had received. Suddenly, while thinking of the Peshwa's nobles, I thought of the Peshwa himself, and remembered the deadly offence I had given him. Then it all became clear. It was by the orders of no less a person than the Peshwa that I had first been shot at by the shikari and afterwards seized as a captive. In the midst of such thoughts we came to a less rugged path, and the smoother motion of the palanquin rocked me to sleep.

"When I was awakened by the cessation of the motion of the palanquin, it was broad daylight. The door or shutter was presently opened, and I was carried out into the light of day. Our halting-place was in a grove of trees, which allowed me no glimpse of the surrounding country. The bonds were taken off my arms and I was given some refreshment, which was comforting as an evidence that there was no immediate intention of murdering me. I tried to enter into conversation with the leader of my captors, but he would give me no information. After a halt of about an hour I was replaced in the palanquin, and we resumed our journey.

"Having proceeded some miles over level ground, we began to go uphill, and continued to do so for such a long time that it became evident to me that we were ascending a mountain of considerable height. The bearers of the palanquin puffed and groaned under my weight, and it was two hours before we reached the summit.

CHAPTER XXVII

JOHN HANNAY'S STORY CONTINUED

WHEN we got to the top of the mountain, the door of the palanquin was once more opened, and I was allowed to look round me. We were on the top of a high mountain, fortified by walls, except where the rocks were so precipitous that artificial fortifications were unnecessary. We looked back upon another still larger mountain to the east, separated from us by a deep valley. Both mountains had more or less level tops, which were covered with dense forests of jambul and other evergreen trees.

"My captors here handed me over to the charge of a Maratha official, who turned out to be the commandant of the fort. They gave him a letter containing written instructions as to how I was to be disposed of. After a short halt at the edge of the mountain, the commandant took me a mile or two along the level top of the mountain to the room that was destined to be my prison for a year. It was in the upper story of a building over the southern bastion of the fort."

"You need not describe it to me," I said, "for I have already been in it and seen the works of art with which you decorated the walls." I then told him how we had scaled Prabul in search of him, and arrived in his prison chamber on the very day on which he had quitted it.

"Well, you need not laugh at my poor attempts at wall decoration," he said. "A prisoner must find some occupation to divert his mind, or he will go mad. Often the commandant of the fort would pay me a visit, and, as he was lively and talkative, I was always glad when he came to see me. He made no secret of the instructions he had received from Poona. He was not ashamed to tell me that the Peshwa had given orders that I should either be killed or captured. Accordingly, the leader of the band sent to carry out his high commands had first made the shikari attempt to assassinate me, and then, when the treacherous shot did not take effect, had fallen upon me in the dark. The commandant did not seem to think that there was anything out of the way in a great prince ordering the assassination or capture of the officer of a foreign nation with which he was ostensibly in alliance. However, the commandant was a good-humoured fellow, and made me as comfortable as possible under the circumstances. His orders were to imprison me on the west side of Prabul, in a cell from the window of which I could see the ships and houses of my countrymen in Bombay, so that, like Dives in the Gospel, I might be tortured by the clear sight of happiness beyond my reach. But there were no buildings on that side of the hill, so the commandant imprisoned me in the room that you saw, and carried out the spirit of the Peshwa's orders by making me walk, under a guard, every day to the western side of the mountain. In this way the Peshwa's ingenuity in devising mental torture conduced to my welfare; for my daily walk of a mile or two was capital exercise, which proved very conducive to my bodily health. Also, the mountain air that blows over the summit of Prabul is cool and exhilarating. So I kept my spirits up, and had good hopes of somehow obtaining release from my captivity, and consequently the sight of the ships in the harbour and the houses of Bombay inspired hope rather than despair.

"Such, then, has been my life for the past year. Every morning I was walked over to the west of the mountain to have my daily view of Bombay. Through the day I worked away at my stone-carving with a blunt carpenter's tool with which the commandant of the fort kindly supplied me. My hussar's uniform was taken away, and was probably hung up as a trophy in the commandant's room. In its place I was given these uncouth but comfortable garments, which were made for me, under my instructions, by a native tailor. When, towards the end of the year, it became cold on the hill-top, especially at night, they presented me with a coarse woollen garment, something like a Highland plaid, except that, instead of being striped, it was of a dusky brown colour throughout.

"I tried to bribe the commandant to come over to the British side, and take me to Bombay. He rejected my offer, declaring that he would never desert his master the Peshwa and the national cause. I respected him for his loyalty, although it stood in the way of my escape from captivity.

"Thus the weeks and months passed away, and I heard few tidings of what was going on in the outer world. At last, yesterday morning, the commandant came and told me that he had orders to join a Maratha force, collecting at Chauk, with his whole garrison, and that I must accompany him. Thus it was that when you entered my prison you found the prisoner gone."

"But how", I asked, "did you escape out of the hands of the Marathas and gain possession of the fine palanquin in which I find you riding in state?"

"The Marathas marched me on with them some miles or so along a gradual ascent to a village called Campoli, at the foot of the Ghaut. We encamped for the night by a tank, into which, my guards exultingly told me, a British general had been compelled to throw his guns in order that they might not be captured by the pursuing Marathas. There seemed to be no order observed in the encampment. Every man did what seemed right in his own eyes. Five men were appointed to guard me; but when some excitement arose in a distant part of the camp, four of them rushed off to see what was going on, leaving only one man to watch their prisoner. This was too good an opportunity to be neglected. When my solitary warder turned his head in the direction of the disturbance, I slipped up behind him, and with a log of firewood gave him such a blow on the skull that he fell stunned, or perhaps dead. Luckily we were at the edge of the camp, so that there was no one to intercept me in my rush to the jungle. One or two Marathas from a distance saw me run off, but did not take the trouble to raise the hue and cry and follow me, thinking, perhaps, that I was only a camp-follower running off to catch a stray donkey.

"When I had got to some distance from the camp I did not venture to take the main road to Chauk, in case I should meet stragglers following the rear of the Maratha force, but traced my course along cattle-tracks through the jungle at some distance from the road. At first my progress was difficult, owing to the darkness, but presently the rising moon enabled me to move on with more safety and speed. After a while I struck a well-beaten track, which appeared to lead from some neighbouring village to

Chauk, and this I followed. I had, however, little hope of escaping recapture. I could not possibly find my way to Bombay except by the main road past Chauk, and as soon as I came to that road I should be likely to meet Maratha soldiers. So with little hope I pressed on until, after walking for an hour or two, I reached a large wood on the outskirts of Chauk. Here, in the tangled light and shade I slipped on the root of a great tree and strained my ankle. What with the pain of my ankle and my weariness I could walk no more. So I threw myself down, utterly exhausted, on the ground, using the dry leaves both as mattress and blanket.

"It was pleasant to lie down to sleep once more as a free man, however short a period my liberty might last. Besides, I was worn out with the excitement of my escape, and with the physical exertion of my hurried flight along rough paths. Whatever might happen, I was thankful to feel sure of one night's undisturbed rest. So I lay down and enjoyed sweet and peaceful sleep until the matin song of the bulbuls in the trees above me announced the approach of dawn. Then I arose, and, having no fixed plan in my mind, followed a mysterious impulse that led me to approach a neighbouring temple, and see what was going on there. In spite of the pain caused by my swollen ankle, I limped up to the wall of the enclosure and looked and listened—not in vain. Just at this moment there came forth from the temple a woman dressed in the orange robe of an ascetic. Under the open sky, now reddening in the east, she stretched forth her hands to heaven and prayed to the god of the temple:

"'Great Mahadev, to whom I have devoted the remainder of my life, hear my prayer and purify my heart, so that I may serve thee worthily and atone for my past wickedness by giving myself up entirely to holy contemplation and good deeds.'

"Hearing these words I advanced, and, throwing myself at her feet, made my prayer to her, saying:

"'Oh, lady! if thou art really beginning a new life in the service of the holy gods, how couldst thou make a better commencement than by holding out thy hand to help a suppliant fugitive, though he be not of thy country or of thy religion. For surely in every religion the great gods tell men to give ear to suppliants and succour the distressed.'

"'Rise up,' she replied, 'and say what thou desirest. Thou art a Feringhi, and every Feringhi has a claim on my gratitude for the sake of one who once braved in my defence the greatest prince in India," and then, as I raised my face, she gave a cry of astonishment, which she smothered immediately, exclaiming: 'John Hannay! Is it thus we meet again, and am I at last given a chance of paying the debt of gratitude I owe thee? Dost thou not remember the unhappy Hira whom thou didst so bravely defend against the violence of the mighty Peshwa a year ago? Tell me quickly why thou appearest in this strange garb, and what I can do to help thee? If thy life be in danger, and I can save it by giving my life, the sacrifice would be no sacrifice, but the greatest joy my unhappy life has ever experienced. But tell me quickly, for the light of day is spreading over the earth, and may reveal thee to thy enemies!'

"Thus adjured I told her in a few words of my escape from captivity, and asked her if she could help me to get to my friends in Bombay.

"'Oh that I had the wit of Namdeo,' she said, 'to devise some means of saving thee! What can I do?' Then, striking her brow, she exclaimed suddenly, with a look of radiant joy: 'I have it! Go and hide thyself again in that clump of trees, and get into the palanquin that will be sent to thee. The bearers will carry thee swiftly to Bombay, and will pretend that they are conveying a lady of the Peshwa's court to Mahad. And now farewell, farewell, farewell! Henceforth I must try to banish thy image from a heart devoted to the service of the great god Mahadev.'

"As she spoke, either by accident or design the part of her yellow robe that had hitherto shrouded her head like a cowl fell down to her shoulders, and I once more saw clearly the face of her whom I had seen as a lovely girl near Chinchwad. The year that had passed since then had changed her, but enhanced rather than impaired her great beauty. A wild light of passion shone in her dark eyes, which carried me away, so that I cried out:

"'Why sacrifice such beauty as thine to the service of a god who is, after all, but a dumb idol? Rather come with me over the sea and trust thy future happiness to my love, which will never fail. Quick, decide, and leave not my heart desolate!'

"'Nay,' she said. 'This yellow robe shows that my choice is already made. If I broke my vow, the power of the great god would stretch his arm across the sea and exact a terrible vengeance. So farewell again, and delay no longer, lest thy pursuers should come upon thee and perchance slay thee before my eyes.'

"So I tenderly kissed her hand and proceeded to limp back to my hiding in the wood, as she had told me to do. When she saw the pain with which I put my right foot to the ground, womanly sympathy quite overcame the reserve inculcated on Hindu women from their earliest years. She expressed the deepest sorrow at what I suffered, and made me sit me down on the turf by the wayside, where she skilfully bound my ankle with a strip of cloth torn from her yellow robe. When I assured her that I was feeling better, she left me, saying:

"'Since thou art too lame to go to the palanquin, I must send the palanquin to thee. And now, once more and forever, farewell, and may the gods in heaven ever bless thee!'

"With these words she went away, and I saw her no more.

"I had not waited long when this palanquin was brought along by these bearers. They salaamed[1] me, and drew aside the curtains, and I stepped in. As they bore me past the temple, I thought I had a glimpse of a yellow robe behind a tree outside the enclosure. Perhaps it was fancy, but, in case it should not be so, I waved my hand from the palanquin. I thought of the strange destiny that had brought me and Hira together in two great crises of our lives, until the violence of your men and your appearance on the scene turned my thoughts in another direction."

When John Hannay had told his tale, I had an equally long tale to tell to him. Great was his surprise when he heard what an active part Hira had played in determining my destiny also. When he heard

[1] See Appendix, note 11.

of her life at the Peshwa's court, he must in his heart have been glad that she had not taken him at his word and accepted his impetuous offer. He did not, however, say so. He was too loyally grateful for the great service Hira had so recently rendered him to say a word that might seem to disparage her, and many a time in after-years we spoke of the strange way in which this beautiful Hindu lady had first endangered our lives, and then intervened to save my life and prevent John Hannay from being captured.

CHAPTER XXVIII

A CHIVALROUS FOE

JOHN HANNAY had scarcely finished his story when we heard the clatter of a horse's hoofs behind us. I looked back and saw my horse, Moti, ridden at a rapid pace towards us by Narayan, the Pindarrie whom I had chosen out of my band of robbers to be my groom and look after my most precious possession. I was very angry with him for the reckless way in which he was riding his master's horse, but my anger was speedily transformed into gratitude and admiration for his loyalty when the faithful fellow sprang from the saddle, and, throwing himself at my feet, exclaimed:

"Dear master, up and away! Close behind me follows a strong body of well-armed Marathas. Mount quickly, for nothing but the swiftness of your good horse can save you from death or capture."

Very exasperating was the prospect of being

thus wrecked, as it were, in sight of port, of losing all the fruits of our exertions and seeming good fortune just when we appeared to have surmounted every difficulty. In the words of the Roman poet I sighed: "Ibi omnis effusus labor", and then proceeded to ask Narayan whether he had not met the rest of the band whom I had sent on foot to recover their horses.

"I met them on the road," he said, "having started alone with Moti to look for my master. They told me where you were to be found, and I hurried on to let you have your horse as soon as possible, for it is not fitting that a noble sahib like you should walk on your feet. But immediately before I caught sight of you, that band of Marathas came down to the road behind me from a path on the right. Look!" he cried out excitedly; "there they are coming round. Why does not my master mount and ride away? See, they are coming nearer and nearer. It will soon be too late."

"I have a friend in that palanquin," I replied, "whom I cannot abandon to the tender mercy of the enemy. I must be faithful to him even as thou hast been faithful to me. Go and tell the bearers to carry the palanquin at a quick pace along the road to Panwell." He reluctantly obeyed, and, mounting Moti, I waited on the road, with my drawn sword in my hand, to see what would happen next. John Hannay was borne away in the palanquin by the bearers, who paid little heed to his gesticulations and remonstrances.

In the meantime the Maratha band had halted at a distance of about a mile, instead of charging against me immediately and overwhelming me by superior numbers, as I thought they would do. Presently a single horseman detached himself from the mass and cantered up to me, flourishing his sword round his head. When he came near, I inferred from his gay dress, his ornaments, and the trapping of his fine horse, that he belonged to one of the noble Maratha families. He reined up his horse at a distance of ten paces, and in a loud voice called upon me to surrender. I replied in words of defiance, challenging him to cross swords with me there and then before his comrades would come to his assistance.

He accepted the challenge with alacrity, and we were soon busily engaged in exchanging blows. To my chagrin I found out that he was a more expert swordsman than I was. He wielded his weapon with remarkable grace and quickness, and succeeded in drawing first blood by a cut at my left arm, which I was only partially able to parry. It was evident that I was pretty sure to get the worst of it, if the sword-play continued much longer, even though the other Marathas should not come up. So I determined to bring the combat to a speedy conclusion, trusting that chance and the superior weight of myself and my horse might give me the upper hand. I suddenly applied the spur to Moti and rode straight at my opponent, shouting loudly and waving my sword in the most violent and unscientific manner, so as to disconcert him. My rough tactics, which he no doubt regarded as extremely ungentlemanly, proved entirely successful. I managed to get to close quarters without receiving the finishing stroke that he might have delivered, had he been able to remain perfectly calm and collected. The shock drove his horse back on its haunches, and, as the rider tried to preserve his equilibrium, I seized him and by main force tore him from his saddle and threw him to the ground, where he lay stunned.

I was about to dismount and see how much

my fallen foe was hurt, when I was aware of another single horseman riding up. So I kept my saddle and retired a few paces, leaving the new arrival to attend upon the fallen man, who was already showing signs of returning life. His comrade rode past him without paying him much attention. In those lawless and turbulent days, wounds and death were of little account among the Marathas. He then, like his predecessor, called upon me to surrender.

"By overthrowing such a swordsman as Natu," he added, "you have done enough to prove your valour. You may now surrender with honour, and I will take you to the noble Govindrao Gokhle, who will grant your life, Feringhi though you be."

I now knew that the leader of the Maratha troop was none other than the generous friend to whom I was indebted for the good horse I rode. In a moment I perceived that it was through his chivalry that the Maratha cavaliers were coming one by one to cross swords with me, instead of overpowering me by superior numbers, as they might so easily have done. The whole proceeding struck me as so knightly that in imagination I was transported to the days of old, and it flashed across my mind that I would try against my new adversary a device that I had read of in the autobiography of that famous Elizabethan philosopher and knight-errant, Lord Herbert of Cherbury, and see if I could *gagner la croupe* of my opponent. I answered his defiance by telling him that I would never disgrace myself by surrendering with weapons in my hand. Immediately he set spurs to his horse and charged along the road straight at me. Instead of awaiting the shock face to face, I turned Moti sideways and backed him to the left side of the road out of the path of my adversary, who did not detect my manœuvre in time to foil it by pulling up his horse. Thus he was borne past Moti's head by the impetus of the charge, and I happily succeeded in gaining the croup of my enemy, which proved as advantageous as gaining the weather-gauge is in a naval combat between two ships at sea. For by advancing upon the hind-quarter of his horse at the right moment I was able to deliver a blow on the Maratha's shoulder from behind which he was utterly unable to parry. I dealt the blow with such force that my sword broke against my enemy's collar-bone. He rode on with his sword-arm hopelessly disabled, while I remained victorious on the spot, holding in my hand the hilt of my sword, with only a few jagged inches of the blade still adhering to it.

In spite of the severe wound that he had received, the Maratha, with his left hand and the pressure of his knees, managed to turn his horse out of the road, and proceeded to ride round by a circuitous path to rejoin his captain and his comrades. Very foolishly, instead of riding after the palanquin to borrow his sword from Narayan, I stood where I was, watching the Maratha as he rode over the rugged ground, and wondering how long it would be before he swooned from loss of blood and fell to the ground. As I stood thus at gaze, for the third time I heard the clatter of a horse's hoofs on the road from Chauk. Almost before I had time to turn tail, my new adversary was upon me. His splendid arms and noble bearing showed me immediately that I had now to do with Gokhle himself. With no weapon but a broken sword in my hand I had to defend myself against one who was reputed to be the best horseman and the most skilful swordsman in Maharashtra. There was little likelihood, indeed, of my emerging successfully out of such a conflict.

Gokhle began, like the other two, by summoning me to surrender.

"Give up your arms," he cried, "and the lady in the palanquin, whom you have defended so valiantly, and in the name of the great Peshwa, whose servant I am, I promise you your life."

Then, suddenly recognizing me, he added:

"What! MacCulloch Sahib! Is it here we meet again? It would be a joy and an honour," he was pleased to say, "to cross swords with you. But I see your sword is broken, and we cannot well fight with one sword between us. What is to be done? If my followers see me let you go free without a struggle, they may report it to my dishonour at the Peshwa's court. Yet I cannot attack an unarmed man, especially one who is my friend. I have it!" he said. "I pray you by the gods do as I tell you!"

So saying, he rode up to me brandishing his sword in hostile fashion. When he came close up to me, he said:

"Now embrace me, but let our embrace be like the grasp of foes engaged in mortal combat."

I did so, and as we swayed to and fro in

what would seem to spectators at a distance a mortal combat, he whispered to me: "Give me your sword and take mine."

I complied with his request, and, like Hamlet and Laertes, we changed our weapons in the scuffle. Finally he said:

"Now, let me go. I will tell my followers that in the fight my sword broke, and that when I was at your mercy you granted me my life on condition that you should be allowed to go on your way unmolested."

I saw no reason why I should not again comply with his request. Gokhle appeared to have a fancy for assuming the character of Horace's *splendide mendax*. Afterwards, when he told me the story of the part he had played at the battle of Kirki, I found that the same feature of his character had been displayed by him on that occasion also. So I unloosed my arms from his body, and with grateful thanks for his chivalrous conduct, to which I owed the life and liberty of myself and my friend, I let him go. He rode off with my broken sword, and I did not see him again until the end of the war.[1]

This was our last adventure. The Marathas

[1] See Appendix, note 12.

disappeared in the jungle by the side of the road, and we were soon after overtaken by my Pindarrie followers, who escorted us safely to Panwell, and thence we sailed in boats across the creek and harbour to Bombay.

CHAPTER XXIX

CONCLUSION

WHEN we arrived at Bombay, my uncle gave us a most hearty reception. He insisted upon paying out of his own purse all that I had promised to my Pindarrie followers, and a little more. Most of them enlisted in British-Indian regiments, and I have no doubt proved good soldiers, or, in the expressive Indian phrase, "true to their salt". The wily Haibati also came in for a liberal reward, under the influence of which he gave us information that he had withheld before. He brought before us evidence to show that Captain Moore had sold secrets of the British Government to the Peshwa. He also asserted that Captain Moore had suggested to the Peshwa the good opportunity that the shooting expedition afforded of taking vengeance on John Hannay; his private motive being to get rid of a creditor to whom he owed a large sum of money. The evidence given by

Haibati against Captain Moore bore the test of cross-examination, and even John Hannay, in spite of his disinclination to believe in the treachery of one who had been his friend, could not help giving credit to the serious charges made against him. We determined to accuse him openly of treachery to his friend and his country when we returned to England, so that he might have an opportunity of clearing his character. But we never had a chance of carrying out our intention; for about this time he made a hurried departure from England, leaving his debts unpaid, and we next heard of him as an officer in the Russian army.

John Hannay left Bombay for home in December, soon after the annual St. Andrew's feast had been celebrated with my uncle in the chair, and arrived safely at Rusko, to the great joy of his father and sister. Old Sir John seemed to renew his youth, when his son, whom he had so long mourned as dead, was restored to him. Alice expressed her sentiments to me in a letter, for I had to remain in India with my regiment until the end of the war. The praise she gave me was no doubt more than I deserved, seeing that the release of her brother was as much due to good fortune and the help of others, especially of Hira, as to my own exertions. Nevertheless, it was the sweetest praise I ever received in my life; and sweetest of all was the conclusion of her letter, in which she told me that, if I had not in the meantime transferred my allegiance to some Indian beauty, she was ready to give me her hand and her heart, and would try to be a good wife to me in India, or England, or wherever else fortune might lead us.

The war kept me in India until the Peshwa surrendered in the year following, and was allowed, by the generosity of Sir John Malcolm, a princely pension, the savings from which were destined to work us woe forty years afterwards in the hands of his adopted son, the infamous Nana Sahib. I was present at the battle of Ashta, where Gokhle once more showed his generalship by directing a charge at the weakest point of the hostile British array. At this battle, too, again was manifested the contrast between his valour and the want of resolution on the part of his followers and his master. Gokhle led in person a gallant charge against the British dragoons, and fell sword in hand, after wounding a British officer and several men, while Baji Rao, at the very beginning of the encounter, jumped out of his palanquin and fled on a swift horse that was kept ready for him in case of danger. My friend, Govindrao Gokhle, also took part in the battle in which his father fell, and was made captive while bravely fighting by his father's side. After the war was over I was happily successful in my efforts to regain for him the favour of the British Government, which his father had formerly enjoyed and forfeited by his devotion to Baji Rao and the national cause. I had no doubt that he and his descendants would adapt themselves to the new state of affairs, and prove faithful servants of the British Government, as being the only power able to give peace and prosperity to a land long distracted by misrule and continual civil war.

It was not until the winter of 1818 that I was able to get leave to return home. It is impossible for me to describe the joy of my home-coming. This was, alas! the last time that I was fated to see the two family circles of Rusko and Castramont unbroken. Soon after my return Alice and I were united in marriage. John Hannay retired from the army to help his father in the management of the estate, to the inheritance of which he was too soon to succeed. The army was my life-long profession. My dear wife accompanied me to India, and was my joy and comfort during the long years of my military service in that country. Often we beguiled the arid heat of the tropics by talking together of the green fields, cool streams, and dewy moorland of grey Galloway, and when I retired from service a few years before the outbreak of the Mutiny, it was in the dearly-beloved valley of the Fleet that we made a home for ourselves and our children.

APPENDIX

Note 1, on p. 54

David MacCulloch was a real person. For an account of his eccentricities, see James Douglas's *Bombay and Western India*, vol. ii, pp. 118, 119. His father knew Burns, and told Lockhart a sad story of the latter days of the great poet, how, "riding into Dumfries one fine summer's evening to attend a country ball, he saw Burns walking alone on the shady side of the principal street of the town, while the opposite part was gay with successive groups of gentlemen and ladies, all drawn together for the festivities of the night, not one of whom seemed willing to recognize the poet. The horseman dismounted and joined Burns, who, on his proposing to him to cross the street, said: 'Nay, nay, my young friend, that's all over now', and quoted, after a pause, some verses of Lady Grizzel Baillie's pathetic ballad—

"'His bonnet stood ance fu' fair on his brow,
His auld ane looked better than mony ane's new;
But now he lets 't wear ony way it will hing,
And casts himself dowie upon the corn-bing.

"'O, were we young, as we ance hae been,
We sud hae been galloping down on yon green,
And linking it owre the lily-white lea,—
And werena my heart light, I wad die.'"

Note 2, on p. 65

The cow is so sacred in the eyes of a Hindu, that to kill a cow is regarded in India as one of the most horrible acts of sacrilege that a man can commit. The sacred character of the cow was no doubt originally due to the recognition of the usefulness of this animal to man.

Note 3, on p. 65

Tulasi Das was a celebrated Brahman poet who flourished in the reigns of Akbar and Jahangir, and died at Benares in 1623. For the wearing away of metal by skin compare Lucretius' verse:—

"Annulus in digito subtertenuatur habendo".

Note 4, on p. 83

"The unshaken constancy of Sukaram Hurry to his master, Rugoba, deserved a better fate. He was chained in irons so heavy that, although a very powerful man, he could scarcely lift them; his food and water were insufficient to allay his hunger or to quench his thirst; but he survived fourteen months; and when so emaciated that he could not rise, 'My strength is gone and my life is going,' said the dying enthusiast, 'but when voice and breath fail, my fleshless bones shall still shout Rugonath Rao! Rugonath Rao!'" (Grant Duff's *History of the Marathas.*) Rugoba, or Rugonath Rao, was the father of Baji Rao.

Note 5, on p. 124

In India the birth of a daughter is generally regarded as a misfortune. To avoid the expense of maintaining and marrying them, female infanticide was commonly resorted to in India before the British conquest, especially among the Rajputs. This view of daughters is expressed in a proverb in Dr. Fallon's collection: "A humiliating portion daughters are; their coming makes you weep, and their going also makes you weep".

Note 6, on p. 134

Clisthenes of Sicyon invited all who wished to marry his daughter to pay him a visit. He entertained them for a year, during which they competed against one another in all kinds of trials of physical and mental excellence. "When at length the day arrived which had been fixed for the espousals, and Clisthenes had to speak out and declare his choice, he first of all made a sacrifice of a hundred oxen, and held a banquet whereat he entertained all the suitors and the whole people of Sicyon. After the feast was ended, the suitors vied with each other in music and in speaking on a given subject. Presently, as the drinking advanced, Hippoclides, who quite dumfoundered the rest, called aloud to the flute-player, and bade him strike up a dance; which the man did, and Hippoclides danced to it. And he fancied that he was dancing excellently well; but Clisthenes, who was observing him, began to misdoubt the whole business. Then Hippoclides, after a pause, told an attendant to bring in a table; and when it was brought, he mounted upon it and danced first of all some Laconian figures, then some Attic ones; after which he stood on his head upon the table and began to toss his legs about. Clisthenes, notwithstanding that he now loathed Hippoclides for a son-in-law by reason of his dancing and his shamelessness, still, as he wished to avoid an outbreak, had restrained himself during the first and likewise during the second dance; when, however, he saw him tossing his legs in the air, he could no longer contain himself, but cried out, 'Son of Tisander, thou hast danced thy wife away!' 'What does Hippoclides care?' was the other's answer. And hence the proverb arose." (Rawlinson's *Herodotus.*)

Note 7, on p. 146

Oh! then as diamond shining bright,
Or emerald dazzling all men's sight,
Unmatched in valour and in might,
    Did Gokleh's fame aspire.
Lone as the moon which, far and high,
Majestic rose through midnight sky,
While never a lesser light is nigh,
And gods in heaven his praises cry,
    His single force upheld
His master's throne, his country's fame,
While lakhs on lakhs,—oh! day of shame,
    His feeble hosts were quelled.
The craven prince had boasted loud
To lead his men to victory proud,
    But soon he turned his head,
And fast to Mhowlee fled away,
While Gokleh still maintained the day,
    And vainly fought and bled.

Note 8, on p. 168

Æneas, having landed in Thrace with the intention of founding a city, cut some boughs to shade the altar of Jupiter. What then happened he relates to Dido, in verses translated by Dryden, as follows:—

"I pulled a plant—with horror I relate
A prodigy so strange and full of fate—
The rooted fibres rose; and from the wound
Black bloody drops distill'd upon the ground.
Mute and amaz'd my hair with terror stood;
Fear shrunk my sinews and congeal'd my blood.
Mann'd once again, another plant I try;
That other gush'd with the same sanguine dye."

It turned out that the blood belonged to Polydorus, a son of Priam, murdered by the Thracian king and buried there. Æneas left the place after erecting a tomb and altar to his ghost. A similar prodigy is related in the first book of Spenser's *Faerie Queene.*

Note 9, on p. 181

Sleeman, in his *Rambles and Recollections*, gives several legends relating how whole armies were put to rout by hornets sent against them by gods to punish acts of sacrilege, and confirms the wonderful account given of the hornets' prowess from his own experience. "I have seen", he writes, "six companies of infantry, with a train of artillery, all put to the rout by a single nest of hornets, and driven off some miles with all their horses and bullocks. . . . I should mention that these hornets suspend their nests to the branches of the highest trees, under rocks, or in old deserted temples." From this fact it would appear that what Sleeman calls hornets were really bees, probably bees belonging to the species called *Apis dorsata*, described in the *Fauna of British India* as "the large bee which, when disturbed, attacks men or animals". For the hornet constructs its nest *in* hollow trees or *in* the ground, while the *Apis dorsata*, according to the *Fauna of British India*, builds nests "on the undersides of the branches of large trees, in caves or underhanging rocks, in buildings, &c.".

Note 10, on p. 191

When Sir Patrick Gray came to Thrieve Castle with a letter from King James II, requiring the Earl of Douglas to give up Maclellan, the tutor of Bombie, whom he had imprisoned, Douglas, as we read in Scott's *Tales of a Grandfather*, received him just as he had arisen from dinner, and, with much apparent civility, declined to speak with Gray on the occasion of his coming until Sir Patrick also had dined, saying, "It was ill talking between a full man and a fasting". But this courtesy was only a pretence to gain time to do a very cruel and lawless action. Guessing that Sir Patrick Gray's visit respected the life of Maclellan, he resolved to hasten his execution before opening the king's letter. Thus, while he was feasting Sir Patrick with every appearance of hospitality, he caused his unhappy kinsman to be led out and beheaded in the courtyard of the castle. After dinner, with the greatest politeness of manner, Douglas led Sir Patrick Gray to the courtyard, where the body of Maclellan was lying, and said: "Sir Patrick, you have come a little too late. There lies your sister's son—but he wants the head. The body is, however, at your service."

Note 11, on p. 216

To salaam, in the dialect of Anglo-Indians, is to touch the forehead respectfully with one's fingers. This action is usually accompanied by the utterance of the word "salaam", meaning "peace", which is the ordinary word of greeting in the East to-day, as it was in the days of the Apostles and long before. Meleager, a Greek writer of epigrams, who was a native of Gadara in Palestine shortly before the Christian era, concluded an imaginary epitaph with the following words:—"If you are a Syrian, Salaam; if you are a Phœnician, Naidios; and if a Greek, Chaire". From this it is plain that the greeting of "peace", so often used by Christ and His apostles, was expressed in the familiar word "salaam". (See 1 Samuel xxv, 6; Psalms xxviii, 3; Micah iii, 5; Matthew x, 13; John xiv, 27; and Hebrews vii, 2. "King of Salem, which is king of peace.")

Note 12, on p. 226

If any English reader should be disposed to think an Oriental warrior incapable of such chivalry as I have attributed to Vamanrao Gokhle, let him read Duraid's story of his encounter with Rabiah, as told in the notes to Lyall's *Ancient Arabian Poetry*. Duraid, with a body of horsemen, saw Rabiah riding in company with a lady mounted on a camel. So he said to one of his horsemen, "Go forward to him, and call out to him, bidding him let the woman go and save himself." The horseman did as he commanded, and was slain by Rabiah. Two other horsemen, who were sent successively on the same errand, were likewise slain. But in the third encounter Rabiah broke his spear in the body of his enemy. Now Duraid began to be much perplexed at the long time that had passed without his men returning, and he rode out himself after Rabiah. And he passed by his horsemen lying slain, and came upon Rabiah riding without any spear. And Duraid called out to him, "Sir knight, such an one as thou is not to be slain. But my horsemen will be taking vengeance for their fellows; and I do not see in thy hand any spear—and thou art young. Take, then, this spear of mine; I will return to my people and withhold them from meddling with thee." And Duraid returned to his companions, and said to them, "The lady's knight has defended her, and slain your fellows and torn my spear out of my hand; there is no prospect of gain to you from him." And Duraid and his people returned home.

I strongly advise my readers to possess themselves of Lyall's *Ancient Arabian Poetry*, and read therein the poem that Duraid composed in praise of his enemy's prowess, and how the lady whom Rabiah so well defended afterwards requited Duraid for his generosity, and the whole story of Duraid and his wisdom and his might until he was slain fighting against the new faith of Mahomet at the battle of Hunain, when he was nearly a hundred years old.